Politics

Politics

Peter Joyce

TEACH YOURSELF BOOKS

For UK order queries: please contact Bookpoint Ltd, 78 Milton Park, Abingdon, Oxon OX14 4TD. Telephone: (44) 01235 400414, Fax: (44) 01235 400454. Lines are open from 9.00–6.00, Monday to Saturday, with a 24 hour message answering service. Email address: orders@bookpoint.co.uk

For U.S.A. & Canada order queries: please contact NTC/Contemporary Publishing, 4255 West Touhy Avenue, Lincolnwood, Illinois 60646–1975, U.S.A. Telephone: (847) 679 5500, Fax: (847) 679 2494.

British Library Cataloguing in Publication Data
A catalogue record for this title is available from The British Library.

Library of Congress Catalog Card Number: On file

First published in UK 2001 by Hodder Headline Plc, 338 Euston Road, London, NW1 3BH.

First published in US 2001 by NTC/Contemporary Publishing, 4255 West Touhy Avenue, Lincolnwood (Chicago), Illinois 60646–1975 USA

Cover photo from Mike Stones

Typeset by Transet Limited, Coventry, England.
Printed in Great Britain for Hodder & Stoughton Educational, a division of Hodder Headline Plc, 338 Euston Road, London NW1 3BH by Cox & Wyman Ltd, Reading, Berkshire.

Impression number 10 9 8 7 6 5 4 3 2 1
Year 2005 2004 2003 2002 2001

Contents

Introduction

Welcome to the **Teach Yourself 101 Key Ideas** series. We hope that you will find both this book and others in the series to be useful, interesting and informative. The purpose of the series is to provide an introduction to a wide range of subjects, in a way that is entertaining and easy to absorb.

Each book contains 101 short accounts of key ideas or terms which are regarded as central to that subject. The accounts are presented in alphabetical order for ease of reference. All of the books in the series are written in order to be meaningful whether or not you have previous knowledge of the subject. They will be useful to you whether you are a general reader, are on a pre-university course, or have just started at university.

We have designed the series to be a combination of a text book and a dictionary. We felt that many text books are too long for easy reference, while the entries in dictionaries are often too short to provide sufficient detail. The **Teach Yourself 101 Key Ideas** series gives the best of both worlds! Here are books that you do not have to read cover to cover, or in any set order. Dip into them when you need to know the meaning of a term, and you will find a short, but comprehensive account which will be of real help with those essays and assignments. The terms are described in a straightforward way with a careful selection of academic words thrown in for good measure!

So if you need a quick and inexpensive introduction to a subject, **Teach Yourself 101 Key Ideas** is for you. And incidentally, if you have any suggestions about this book or the series, do let us know. It would be great to hear from you.

Best wishes with your studies!

Paul Oliver
Series Editor

Dedication

To my wife, Julie, and my daughters, Emmeline and Eleanor

Accountability

Accountability (which is often referred to as responsibility) denotes that an individual or organisation to whom power has been delegated is required to submit to the scrutiny of another body or bodies to answer for the actions that have been undertaken. Additionally, the body to whom the organisation or individual is answerable possesses sanctions should actions be undertaken which are deemed to be unacceptable.

There are two forms of accountability. The individual or organisation may have to seek prior permission before taking actions. Alternatively, accountability may entail an individual or organisation being free to take actions but required to report what has been done to another body. This is termed *ex post facto* accountability.

In liberal democratic political systems governments are accountable to the electorate. While in office they may take decisions but the electorate has the ultimate ability to remove them from power at a national election. Elections thus enable the public to exert influence over the legislative and executive branches of government and hold them accountable for their actions. Effective accountability also requires that citizens are in possession of information by which to judge the activities undertaken by public officials. Many liberal democracies provide for this through freedom of information legislation.

Additionally, governments in liberal democratic political systems are accountable to legislatures. They may be required to submit their policies to the scrutiny of legislative bodies, and in parliamentary forms of government legislatures possess the ability to remove the government by passing a vote of 'no confidence' in it. Members of legislative bodies are accountable to their constituents (who possess the power not to re-elect them) and also to their political party which may exercise sanctions such as de-selection or expulsion.

see also...

Elections; Freedom of information; Liberal democracy; Parliamentary system of government; Participation; Political party

Adversarial politics

Adversarial politics is a situation in which one party is automatically disposed to oppose the views and suggestions of another. Parties are thus more concerned to 'score points off each other' than to promote the national interest. Politics in the United Kingdom are traditionally conducted in this manner.

One danger with this situation is that a political party may oppose all the actions of its opponents on principle. Thus, when the governing party is defeated at a general election and is replaced in office by one of its opponents, the latter may devote much of its initial period of government in reversing the policies pursued by its predecessor.

Adversarial politics may mean that legislatures lack any sense of common purpose. Its work is less concerned with a search for the best solutions to national problems and instead is activated mainly by the furtherance of partisan acrimony and the pursuit of party advantage. Members of the legislature who support the executive are likely to back that government and deride proposals made by the opposition party (or parties) regardless of the merits of the cases put forward. Similarly, those who are not supporters of the government are likely to make destructive rather than constructive assessments of initiatives put forward by the executive branch. This may affect the way in which members of the public feel towards the legislature if it is viewed as an institution whose main function is to play party politics rather than advance national concerns.

Adversarial politics may be influenced by electoral systems since coalition government (often a feature of proportional representation) may promote consensus politics (the opposite of adversarial politics) whereas the first-past-the-post system of voting often facilitates a government formed by one party that does not consider the views of other political parties.

see also...

Adversarial politics; Coalition government; Consensus politics; First-past-the-post system of voting; Ideology; Proportional representation

Affirmative action

Affirmative action (or 'positive discrimination') refers to a programme of measures designed to give preferential treatment to certain groups that have historically been disadvantaged as the result of discrimination. Such groups may include racial minorities who suffer from problems including social and economic deprivation, but may also embrace other minorities such as the physically handicapped, homosexuals or lesbians who have been the victims of popular prejudice which has affected such issues as employment opportunities.

Affirmative action is more radical than equal opportunity programmes. The latter seek to ensure that members of disadvantaged groups do not experience discrimination in areas such as job applications or interviews. Affirmative action, however, seeks to ensure that positive steps are taken to guarantee that members of disadvantaged groups can gain access to facilities such as jobs, housing and education. One means of securing this is through the use of quotas: this would ensure, for example, that in an area in which 25% of the population were from an Afro-Caribbean background, employment opportunities would reflect this.

Affirmative action programmes were initiated in America by the 1964 Civil Rights Act. Title VI of the Act prohibited discrimination under any programme that received any federal financial assistance and Title VII made it illegal to discriminate in employment matters.

To be effective, affirmative action needs to be underpinned by strong sanctions that may be applied against those who discriminate against disadvantaged groups. In America the courts may hear class actions (that is, an application on behalf of an entire group that alleges discrimination which, if successful, will result in all members being compensated). However, critics of this approach believe that failing to treat all members of society equally can result in injustices. The new right believed that the position of disadvantaged minorities would be enhanced through the expanding economy rather than affirmative action programmes.

see also...

New Right; Racism

Agenda setting

Agenda setting refers to the ability to determine which issues receive the attention of policy makers. In a positive sense it refers to placing demands before policy makers which they feel obliged to consider but it also has a negative aspect which entails excluding issues from their consideration.

Demands directed at policy makers derive from a number of sources. At national government level they may derive from politicians, civil servants or pressure groups. Decisions made by the courts may influence a political agenda and the operations of specific government departments or agencies may affect the operations of other branches of the bureaucracy. Many issues regularly appear on policy agendas, although a crisis may sometimes result in a new issue being accorded prominent attention. Placing an issue on an agenda does not, however, mean that policy makers will initiate a course of action since, having considered an issue, they may decide to take no action or delay a decision. A number of factors may determine whether an issue enters onto a policy agenda. These include the extent of popular support urging a particular course of action to be adopted by a government, or the extent to which a demand is endorsed by political parties or organisations such as trade unions. Alternatively, other issues may be excluded from policy agendas for reasons such as complexity, a perception that a solution is difficult or impossible to implement or the lack of political clout by those pressing for action to be taken.

The media exert a significant role in setting the political agenda. They may publicise a particular concern, seeking to mobilise its readers, listeners or viewers thereby placing pressure on policy makers to resolve the problem. A beneficial aspect of this activity is that the media may lead public opinion in a progressive direction, perhaps securing action on a social problem that would otherwise have been ignored. Alternatively, however, they may whip up mass hysteria against unpopular minority groups and get punitive actions taken against them.

see also...

Bureaucracy; Executive branch of government; Media

Anarchism

Anarchism literally means 'no rule' and is a form of socialism that rejects conventional forms of government on the basis that it imposes restraints on individuals without their express consent having been given. Accordingly, anarchists urge the abolition of the state and all forms of political authority especially the machinery of law and order (which they view as the basis of oppression providing for the exercise of power by some members of society over others). Most anarchists deem violence as the necessary means to tear down the state.

Anarchists assert that government is an unnecessary evil since social order will develop naturally. Cooperation will be founded upon the self-interest of individuals and regulated by their common sense and willingness to resolve problems rationally. They assert that traditional forms of government, far from promoting harmony, are the root cause of social conflict. Private ownership of property, a key aspect of capitalist society, is regarded as a major source of this friction.

Some aspects of Marxism (especially the view that under communism the state would 'wither away') are compatible with anarchist views. Anarchist thought has been concerned with developing social structures outside conventional forms of government in the belief that the elimination of the state would eradicate exploitation and that cooperation, fraternity and a fair division of goods and labour would be facilitated in smaller forms of social organisation. These have included syndicalism (which sought worker control of industry to be achieved by strike action), communes and a wide range of cooperative endeavours (characterised by relatively small groups of individuals owning and operating a productive enterprise that is managed for their mutual economic benefit).

Key anarchist thinkers include the Russians Mikhail Bakunin (1814–1876) and Pëtr Kropotkin (1842–1921). The latter viewed the medieval city as the ideal social unit.

see also...

Capitalism; Communism; Marxism–Leninism; Socialism

Authority

An individual or institution which possesses authority secures compliance to its suggestions because there is general agreement that those who put forward these ideas have the right to propose and implement them. Thus governments which possess authority are able to influence the actions of their citizens because there is a general consensus that it has the right to take decisions even if the content of them is not generally popular.

The sociologist Max Weber (1864–1920) suggested that authority could be derived from one or other of three sources. First, traditional authority where acceptance of the right to rule is based on custom. Popular consent is accorded to decisions made by those from a background which traditionally exercises the functions of government within a state. Hereditary monarchs (who rule by virtue of birth) enjoy this form of authority. Second, charismatic authority, derived from personal characteristics of a political leader. The main criterion for obedience is that the public stand in awe of the person taking decisions. Charisma is particularly associated with dictators, including Adolf Hitler (1899–1945) in Germany and Juan Péron (1895–1974) who served as President of Argentina between 1946–1955 and 1973–1974. The final source was legal-bureaucratic or legal-rational authority. In this case, compliance to decisions made by rulers is based on the office an individual holds within a state and not on his or her personal characteristics. It is thus the prestige accorded by the public to an office that influences the ability of an official to secure acceptance to his or her wishes.

In liberal democratic political systems the political office occupied by those who give orders forms the main basis of their authority. It is accepted that presidents or prime ministers have the right to give orders by virtue of the public positions they occupy. However, political leaders frequently derive their authority from more than one source: in Britain the association of the prime minister with government carried out in the name of the monarch gives this officeholder authority derived from both traditional and legal-bureaucratic sources.

see also...

Elite; Fascism; Marxism–Leninism; Pluralism; Populism; Power

Bicameral legislature

A bicameral legislature is composed of two separate 'houses' or debating chambers. For example, the United Kingdom parliament consists of the House of Commons and the House of Lords, and in America Congress is divided into the House of Representatives and the Senate. The opposite of this arrangement is a unicameral system in which the legislature consists of only one chamber, as is the case in Finland, Denmark, Sweden and Israel.

One benefit of bicameral legislatures is that one chamber can perform the role of a revising chamber. On occasions when legislation is contentious a second chamber can calmly re-evaluate what has been done and invite a reassessment of the situation.

In bicameral systems, the two chambers of the legislature are often composed differently. This enables issues to be examined from different perspectives and frequently entails one chamber representing popular opinion as expressed in elections with the other providing for the representation of the more localised views of the areas, states or regions into which the country is divided. For example, in Germany the *Bundestag* consists of representatives elected by the voters, whereas the *Bundesrat* provides a forum at national level in which the views of the states (or *Länder*) can be put forward. Second chambers may also represent the interests of specific groups within a country. This is referred to as functional representation and is a feature of the composition of the Irish *Seanad*.

One difficulty with bicameral legislatures is how to resolve the disputes that arise between the two chambers to prevent a situation of stalemate arising. This situation may be catered for if a country's constitution establishes the pre-eminence of one of the two chambers. as is the case in the United Kingdom. In America, however, both branches of the legislature are equal in status and disagreements between them are resolved through the a conference committee.

see also...

Elections; Legislative branch of government; Representation

Bureaucracy

A bureaucracy consists of salaried public officials who work in the executive branch of government and whose role is to administer the policies of that government. Many who perform this work are categorised as civil servants.This means that key matters such as recruitment, pay, promotion, grading, dismissal and conditions of work are subject to common regulations that operate throughout the national government. Such common regulations are enforced centrally by bodies such as the American Office of Personnel Management or the United Kingdom Civil Service Commission.

Bureaucracies employ large numbers of people who are employed within government agencies and departments. Efficiency in administration requires rational organisation. Max Weber (1864–1920) suggested that the ideal bureaucracy would be organised according to a number of principles. He suggested that appointments should be determined on the basis of tests and not patronage, that bureaucratic decision making should be characterised by the impersonal application of established rules and procedures (the term 'red tape' being commonly used to describe the consequences of this method of operation), that the structure should be hierarchical with each bureaucrat occupying a defined place in a chain of command and that bureaucracies should operate on the basis of technical expertise.

Civil servants perform a variety of roles in liberal democratic states, but there are two which have traditionally been emphasised. First, they advise on the content of public policy. This task is carried out by the most senior civil servants who in the United Kingdom are collectively referred to as the higher civil service and whose experience in government gives them considerable power in shaping a government's political agenda. Second, they exercise responsibility for policy implementation which involves a wide range of activities including the delivery of a service to the public.

see also...

Agenda setting; Executive branch of government; New public management

Cabinet

The cabinet is a group of senior politicians, presided over by the chief executive, who meet formally to discuss major issues of public policy.

In some countries (such as America) the cabinet is dominated by the president, but in others (such as the United Kingdom) a tradition of cabinet government exists whereby decision making is viewed as a collective activity undertaken by senior politicians. The cabinet was traditionally viewed as a decision making body at the very heart of government, exercising general superintendence over policy, providing cohesion to its affairs and enabling a number of different departmental perspectives to be brought to bear on a common issue.

The vitality of cabinet government has, however, been adversely affected by developments that include decisions being taken outside of cabinet meetings such as cabinet committees (which operate within the framework of the cabinet system) or through the use of informal structures divorced from the structure of the cabinet. These include liaison between ministers or informal groupings centred on the prime minister. This situation may suggest that cabinet government in the United Kingdom has been replaced by prime ministerial government.

The argument that cabinet government has declined, however, is not universally accepted. The style or character of individual prime ministers influences whether they wish to exercise initiative or use the teamwork of cabinet government to decide major policy issues. Prime ministers need to be wary of conduct viewed as overbearing by their cabinet colleagues as resignations can undermine the prime minister's hold on office. Further, the cabinet retains important functions, such as providing a forum for leading members of the government to be made aware of key political issues, presenting the semblance of a unified government involved in collective decision making and acting as a final court of appeal to arbitrate disputes between ministers.

see also...

Executive branch of government; Ministerial responsibility

Capitalism

Capitalism is an economic system in which the means of production, distribution and exchange are in private hands (whom Karl Marx (1818–1883) referred to as the *bourgeoisie*). The basis of this economic system rests on the accumulation of profit by the bourgeoisie, secured through the exploitation of the working class (whom Marx referred to as the *proletariat*). The profit made is then invested. Capitalism also requires the sale and purchase of goods and services to take place within a relatively free and competitive market. The original theory of capitalism was the 'perfect competition model' of economics in which small-scale entrepreneurs hired, at the least possible cost, workers who produced the maximum possible output at the cheapest possible price.

This economic system is distinct from a planned economy in which the means of production, distribution and exchange of goods and services are controlled by the state. This characterises communist countries. In many liberal democracies, however, there exists a mixed economy in which the ownership of the means of production is shared between the state and private sector. This makes the state a major employer and state intervention may extend into areas such as regulating wages, conditions of employment and subsidising loss-making industries in order to sustain a relatively high level of employment.

Belief in the free market was a prominent aspect of 'new right' thinking in the 1980s which sought to reduce the degree of government involvement in economic affairs. The new right wished to ensure that matters such as economic growth and employment opportunities were secured through the 'natural' forces of supply and demand rather than as the result of government intervention in economic affairs. This resulted in deregulation, privatisation and restrictions being placed on trade union activity who were blamed for preventing market forces from operating effectively by insisting, on wage rises unsupported by productivity.

see also...

Communism; Marxism–Leninism; New right; Privatisation

Citizenship

Citizenship refers to the relationship between a political community (historically, the state) and the people who live in it. It seeks to establish a sense of common identity based on the allocation of rights to the people in return for their acceptance of responsibilities. The rights associated with citizenship were initially civil rights and political privileges, most notably the right to vote, which placed on citizens the obligation to participate in the conduct of political affairs. This differentiated citizens from slaves who did not possess such privileges.

Political inclusion, secured by giving the right to vote to increased numbers of people did not, however, succeed in securing the attachment of all members of society to the state since economic and social divisions resulted in the less fortunate experiencing a sense of social exclusion. Increasingly, therefore, citizenship entailed social and economic reforms directed at the poorer members of society which were designed to create a sense of national cohesion and thereby prevent revolutionary action by the poor directed at the rich. In the United Kingdom, the welfare state was created and advanced by Labour and Conservative goverments after 1945 it included entitlements (such as the right to a job, access to a comprehensive national health service and the availability of a range of social welfare benefits) that extended the social and economic aspects of citizenship to increased numbers of people.

Western governments influenced by 'new right' thinking after 1980 shifted the focus of citizenship away from the state provision of a range of services designed to create a unified society and, instead, emphasised the exercise of individual initiative and consumer choice. Those able to take advantage of the opportunities offered by the free market economy constituted the new basis of citizenship and those unable to play any part in its operations were referred to as the 'underclass'.

see also...

Civil rights; Equality; Liberal democracy; New right; Third way; Underclass

Civil rights

Civil rights encompass a range of personal freedoms governing the relationship between the governed and the government of a particular country and are usually embodied in codified constitutions. In America, these are contained in the first ten amendments to the constitution, collectively referred to as the Bill of Rights. These include the freedom of religion, speech and assembly, and the right to petition for the redress of grievances. In Ireland, personal rights such as the equality of all citizens before the law, the right of *habeas corpus* (that is, an obligation not to imprison a person unless this detention is authorised by the courts) and the freedom of expression (including the right to criticise government policy) are embodied in the constitution.

There are, however, limitations to the effectiveness of defending civil rights by constitutional safeguards. Legal discrimination against women persisted for many years in France despite constitutional provisions seeming to outlaw such practices. The former state of West Germany imposed restrictions on the freedom of speech even though the constitution prohibited this.

In the United Kingdom, civil liberties were rooted in common law and were adversely affected by the ability of parliament to pass legislation that limited their scope. The ability to take part in processions or assemblies, for example, was restricted by legislation such as the 1986 Public Order Act and the 1994 Criminal Justice and Public Order Act.

The ability to reduce civil liberties by legislation provided an important argument in favour of the United Kingdom having either a codified constitution or a bill of rights to put citizens' rights on a statutory basis. This approach was adopted by the enactment of the 1998 Human Rights Act. However, this enabled the judiciary to define the scope of civil liberties and it is questionable whether these are adequately defended by subjecting the actions of the legislature or executive to socially unrepresentative, unelected and politically unaccountable judges.

see also...

Constitution; Human rights; Judicial branch of government

Coalition government

Coalition government is one whose members are drawn from representatives of more than one political party. Its main advantage is that the policy carried out by the government is not based on the preferences of only one party but embraces a range of opinions thereby potentially reflecting a broader cross section of public opinion.

There are, however, a number of problems associated with coalition government. It is often depicted as denying the public the ability to determine the composition of government or the policies it pursues (which are instead often determined by deals struck between politicians after an election has taken place). Coalition government is also seen to be weak and unstable in the sense that one of the participant parties may desert the government which then collapses. This problem is often attributed to proportional representation which is alleged to promote the development of a multi-party system. These difficulties were one consideration that prompted Italian voters to move away from proportional representation. Italy has had in excess of fifty governments in the post-war period. Following a referendum to end proportional representation for elections to the senate in 1993, new election rules were introduced under which 75% of the seats in the chamber of deputies were subject to the first-past-the-post system of election. The remaining seats were allocated by the regional party list system of proportional representation.

Proportional representation does not inevitably result in coalition government.The use of the single transferable vote did not prevent the dominance of *Fianna Fail* over Irish government for many years. Further, coalition government is not inevitably weak and unstable. A coalition of the Christian Democratic Union, the Christian-Social Union and the Free Democratic Party provided Germany's government between 1982 and 1998 when it was replaced by a new coalition consisting of the Social Democratic Party and the Greens.

see also...

Elections; First-past-the-post system of voting; Proportional representation; Referendum

Collectivism

Collectivism entails the sacrifice of self-interest to commonly agreed goals. These are often asserted by a central political authority which results in the state taking an active role directing the resources at its command to achieve these objectives.

Collectivism is usually depicted as the opposite of individualism, since group needs are placed above the pursuit of individual interests. However, some aspects of liberal thought argue that these ideas are not incompatible since the sense of cooperation and fraternity which emerges through collective endeavour enables individuals to develop their personalities to a greater extent than would be possible if they existed in isolation.

Collectivism arose in the United Kingdom towards the end of the nineteenth century when various socialist organisations advocated a more vigorous response by the state to social problems, especially poverty, that would entail an enhanced level of government intervention in the economy and some redistribution of resources from the more affluent members of society. Some within the Liberal Party (the 'new Liberals') also moved towards advocating activity by both central and local government to improve social conditions. This resulted in legislation in the early twentieth century to benefit the poorer and weaker members of society which ultimately developed into the welfare state.

Collectivism is traditionally closely identified with socialism, especially those who view state ownership of the means of production (achieved through policies such as nationalisation) as the way to achieve a more just society. However, collective action can be organised through social units other than the state (such as communities possessing a wide degree of political autonomy) and may underpin economic ventures such as cooperatives in which people can work together and pursue common aims within a capitalist economic system. Some anarchists, including Mikhail Bakunin (1814–1876) embrace this form of non state socialism.

see also...

Anarchism; Capitalism; Individualism; Liberalism; Socialism

Colonialism

Colonialism implies that one nation is inferior to another. This situation arises as the result of the process of occupation by one country of another, usually as the result of warfare, and the subsequent control exerted over the conquered country whose inhabitants are politically controlled, economically exploited and culturally dominated by the colonising country.

This term 'colony' originates with settlements established by the Greek city states around 600 BCE. The original usage of the term described a process whereby citizens of one state settled in another country but retained political and constitutional links with their former country which commonly exerted supreme legislative power (including the power to tax) over them.

Subsequently, the term became associated with the occupation of African countries by European powers in the nineteenth century. These countries were then governed by the conquering country and the economies of colonised countries were required to serve the needs of the colonial power by supplying it with raw materials at low prices and to act as a market for the goods the latter produced on terms that were to its advantage. Cultural domination was an important aspect of colonialism. This was justified by arguments that alleged that the conquered peoples were backward and would benefit greatly from their association with the more developed nations of western Europe, whose advantages included Christianity and education. Those subject to colonisation were thus constrained to abandon their culture (and often their language) and adopt those of the colonial power.

The process of colonialism is different from that of imperialism. This also entails one country conquering other nations, but some or all of the citizens of the conquered countries are accorded citizenship. Members of colonised countries, however, are viewed as subject people with few or no political and legal rights.

Colonialism is an integral explanation of the subsequent development of racism, giving rise to perceptions that black people are inferior to whites.

see also...

Dependency; Racism

Communism

Communism (sometimes referred to as socialist democracy) is a political system based on the ideas of Karl Marx (1818–1883). According to Marxist theory, communism occurs following the overthrow of capitalism and after an intermediary phase (referred to as socialism) in which the Communist Party functions as the vanguard of the proletariat, ruling on its behalf and paving the way for the eventual establishment of communism. This is characterised by the abolition of private property and class divisions and the creation of equality in which citizens live in cooperation and harmony. In this situation the state becomes unnecessary and will 'wither away'.

Considerable differences existed between communist states (especially the former USSR and China whose approaches to issues such as social equality were dissimilar) although, in general, these countries were characterised by the existence of little or no private property ownership, a planned economy (viewed as essential to achieving equality and classlessness) and a comprehensive welfare state.

The most notable feature of communist states is the paramount position of an official socialist ideology and the domination or total monopolisation of political affairs by the official Communist Party. As the massacre of opponents to the communist regime in China at Tiananmen Square in 1989 evidenced, dissent is not encouraged in communist states. The control that the Communist Party exerts over government means that the judiciary is less able to defend civil and political liberties as is the case in liberal democratic political systems.

Communist states included the former Soviet Union and its East European satellite neighbours, but following the 'collapse' of communism in eastern Europe between 1989–1991, communism is now confined to a smaller number of countries, including the People's Republic of China, Vietnam, Cuba and North Korea.

see also...

Capitalism; Civil rights; Liberal democracy; Marxism–Leninism; Political system; Socialism; Totalitarian

Confederation

A confederation is a political structure in which a group of nations agrees to cooperate to achieve common aims that are frequently of a defensive or economic nature. It bears some relationship to federalism, the key difference concerning the powers of the national government. In a federal structure the central government has a wide degree of power that may (notably in America) be expanded at the expense of the state governments. By contrast, the national government of a confederation has extremely limited powers, with most tasks of government being performed by those states or countries that are part of it. These retain their sovereignty and their right to secede. A particular feature of a confederation is that the national government has no direct powers over citizens: functions such as taxation and law enforcement are exercised by the constituent governments.

The main difficulties associated with confederations include the absence of a strong central government able effectively to coordinate the actions of its members. These structures are also often dominated by the larger members.

A confederal system of government was established by the American colonies engaged in the War of Independence against Britain. The Articles of Confederation that were drawn up by the Continental Congress in 1777 provided for a confederacy to be known as the United States of America. The 11 Southern States of America which seceded in the Civil War were also subject to this form of government between 1861 and 1865. The Commonwealth of Independent States (CIS) (established in 1991, following the collapse of the Soviet Union) is a more recent creation.

Further examples of confederations are organisations that seek to promote social, political or economic policies in the mutual interests of its members. An example is the North Atlantic Treaty Organisation. Confederations may develop into federal structures (as happened in Switzerland) and there is debate whether the European Union will develop in this way.

see also...

Communism; European Union; Federal system of government

Consensus politics

Consensus politics entails agreeing rival political parties on a number of key issues, including basic political principles, policy and governing arrangements.

Consensus may arise as the result of society not being divided on ideological grounds. In America, for example, support for individualism and personal freedom are widely held values throughout society. However, consensus may occur in countries where ideology traditionally separates the political parties. In the United Kingdom a social democratic consensus emerged after 1945 which involved the Labour and Conservative Parties accepting an expanding role for the state in a range of social and economic affairs. Both parties were agreed on the desirability of a mixed economy, on the need for government action to ensure a high level of employment, and the need for a welfare state to combat social problems. In both the United Kingdom and the United States, consensus was underpinned by a general increase in affluence in the post-war period which was to the benefit of the working class and helped to erode class antagonisms. Consensus came to an end during the 1970s and in the 1980s Conservative governments pursued economic and social policies which were often bitterly opposed by their political rivals. However, many left wing parties began to undertake reforms to their policies and ideology in response to the electoral popularity of 'new right' politics. The New Zealand Labour Party adopted monetarist economic policies after 1984. The actions undertaken by the United Kingdom Labour Party, in government after 1997, were in many respects influenced by the policies of previous Conservative governments. This suggested that Conservative governments had established support for a new consensus which was underlaid by a commitment to a market economy.

However, the extent of consensus may be overstated and may be stronger among political elites than within political opinion in general.

see also...

Adversarial politics; Bureaucracy; New right; Political party; Social democracy

Conservatism

The essence of conservative ideology is sceptical to change. The desire to 'retain things as they are' is especially concerned with what are deemed to be the key institutions and values on which society is based. These include support for private property ownership. This results in opposition to any form of social (including moral) upheaval, support for firm (but not despotic) government and a belief that political institutions should evolve naturally rather than being artifically constructed from an abstract theory or blueprint. Conservatism rejects the goal of equality achieved by social engineering, believing that the differences that exist between people are natural and should not be tampered with. Conservatism is often equated with nationalistic sentiments, seeking to safeguard domestic values and the way of life against foreign incursions.

Conservative thought developed in the eighteenth century and was especially influenced by the events of the French Revolution. Conservatism in the United Kingdom was considerably influenced by *Reflexions on the Revolution in France,* written by Edmund Burke (1729–1797) in 1792. Although he had initially been sympathetic to the French Revolution, he subsequently turned against it when the scale of the destruction of the established order became apparent. He explained this alteration in the direction of his thought by providing a summary of the 'British way' which constituted a classic statement of conservatism. He argued that an Englishman's freedom was a national inheritance that was most effectively secured by government which balanced democracy, aristocracy and monarchy. His defence of traditions and institutions was coupled with the advocacy of evolutionary change. He accepted that change would sometimes be necessary, but advocated that this should be minimal and should seek to preserve as much of the old as was possible. In France, Joseph de Maistre (1753–1851) contributed to conservative thought by providing a defence of established authority against revolutionary ideas and emphasising the need for order.

see also...

Nationalism; New right

Consociationalism

Consociationalism (which is often referred to as power sharing) seeks to provide a stable system of government in a plural society that is characterised by the existence of fundamental divisions (which may be based upon religion, race, language, ideology or culture) and in which other key aspects of civic affairs (such as political parties, pressure groups and the educational system) are organised on the same basis. The groups into which society is divided compete for control of the same territority.

This model for governing divided societies was developed by a Dutch political scientist, Arend Lijphart who wrote *Democracy in Plural Societies*, published in 1977. She put forward four key features of consociational democracy. These were government by a grand coalition of the political leaders of all the significant sections into which society was divided. This entails cooperation by political elites in the formation of an executive branch of government. The second feature was the introduction of a veto which the various sections could use to defend their interests against majority decisions, the third was that political representation should be based on proportional principles. and the final aspect of consociationalism was that each section of society should be granted a high degree of autonomy to regulate its own affairs.

Consociationalism entailing the establishment of a coalition government composed of representatives of various ethnic groups to provide unified government for the territory that they share is practiced in Northern Ireland. The 1998 Northern Ireland Act provided for an assembly and an executive committee drawn from the major parties represented in it.

Various political arrangements may be used to provide autonomy to the groups into which society is divided. A wide element of self-government can be provided by a federal political structure (as is the case in Belgium and Canada) or through a regional structure (as is the case in Spain).

see also...

Coalition government; Devolution; Federal system of government

Constitution

A constitution provides a framework within which a country's system of government is conducted. It contains a formal statement of the composition and powers of the key branches of government, the relationship between them and (in a federal political structure) provides guidance concerning the respective powers of the national and sub national units of government. It typically contain statements concerning the relationship between the government and its citizens which are referred to as civil rights.

In addition to providing information regarding the structure of government, a constitution will also lay down certain ground rules governing the conduct of political activity that are subsequently enhanced by customs and practices (termed 'conventions'). Deviations from these norms may take one of two forms – unconstitutional acts (which contravene either the letter or the spirit of the constitution) and anti-constitutional actions (which display a total disregard for the entire constitutional arrangements and may seek to overthrow them).

There is usually one document that contains information concerning the manner in which a country's system of government operates. Examples of codified documents include the American Constitution of 1787. Codified constitutions have a superior status to ordinary legislation and actions that contravene them may be set aside by the process of judicial review. They are termed 'rigid' which means they can be only amended through a procedure different from the normal law-making process.

The United Kingdom, New Zealand and Israel are examples of countries without codified constitutions. They are described as unwritten in the sense that there is no one single, specific document providing information on their systems of government. Instead such information is scattered across a number of different sources. Uncodified constitutions are typically flexible which means they can be amended through the normal law-making process.

see also...

Civil rights; Federal system of government; Human rights; Judicial review; Separation of powers

Corporatism

Corporatism entails the formation of formal organisations, termed corporations, that bring together diverse groups associated with particular economic activities (such as owners, workers and technical experts) with representatives of the state so that their conflicting interests can be resolved and the national interest advanced. These corporations occupy an intermediary role between the state and its citizens.

Corporatist theory blends elements of pluralism and elitism. In common with pluralism it emphasises the importance of pressure groups in the formulation of public policy, but follows elite theory by emphasising that a dominant position should be occupied by a relatively small number of powerful and highly organised groups that become incorporated into the state's decision making machinery.

Corporatism originated with the formation of trade guilds in medieval times. This form of social organisation was ended by the advent of the Industrial Revolution, but reappeared in the twentieth century in Spain and Italy when governed by the fascist rulers General Francisco Franco (1892–1975) and Benito Mussolini (1883–1945). Interest groups representing capital and labour were incorporated into the machinery of the state which provided the government with the means to control all aspects of economic activity.

In more recent times what is termed 'neo-corporatism' denotes a close working relationship between government, unions and business interests. One example of this was the National Economic Development Council set up in the United Kingdom in 1962 whose key role was to plan for industrial growth. The implications of this were twofold. Legislatures became devalued as key policies were determined in an alternative forum. The public's ability to influence of public policy through elections was diminished since key policy decisions were taken in secretive closed meetings by persons who were unaccountable for their actions.

see also...

Authority; Elite; Fascism; Pluralism; Power; Representation

Dealignment

There are two aspects of dealignment – partisan dealignment and class dealignment.

Partisan dealignment means that a large number of electors either desert the party to which they were traditionally committed or identify with the party which they historically supported far more weakly. A number of factors may explain this phenomenon. These include increased education and political awareness of many members of the electorate (making them prone to basing their vote on logical as opposed to traditional considerations) and perceptions that the party normally supported by an elector does not reflect his or her own views on key isssues. For example, the loss of support experienced by the United Kingdom Labour Party in the early 1980s was attributed to the 'swing to the left' that occurred after the 1979 general election defeat, causing what is termed an 'ideological disjuncture' between the views and values of the party and those of its supporters. Political crises may also influence partisan dealignment. In America between 1958 and 1968 key political issues such as the Vietnam War and Civil Rights Movement resulted in an increased number of voters registering themselves as independents.

Class dealignment suggests that the historic identity between a political party and a particular social class becomes of reduced significance. In the United Kingdom this might be explained after 1970 by the reduced intensity of class consciousness that arose for factors which included the increased affluence of the working class (termed 'embourgeoisement'), the decline in the number of manual workers and the rise in the service sector of employment. This disadvantaged the Labour Party, which failed to win a general election between 1979 and 1997.

Partisan and class dealignment have two main consequences for the conduct of politics. Third parties obtain increased levels of support and the core support given to established major parties is less consistent from one general election to the next.

see also...

Psephology; Realignment

Democracy

Democracy describes a political system in which power resides with the people who live in a particular state: it is they who are sovereign.

Democratic government was initiated in the Greek city state of Athens in the fifth century BC. The word 'democracy' is derived from two Greek words, *demos* (meaning people) and *kratos* (meaning power). The term thus literally means 'government by the people' as opposed to the powers of government being confined to a single ruler or small group of citizens as is the case in an oligarchy. One advantage of democracy is that the ability of all citizens to play a part in decision making may help foster a sense of social solidarity. However, this method of government may result in the views of the majority prevailing over the interests of minorities or result in public policy being based on popular prejudices rather than informed opinion.

Initially, major decisions were taken by meetings open to all free males. This system is referred to as direct democracy. It was possible for government to function in this way when the population was small and the activity of the state limited. Today, however, ancient city states have been replaced by bigger units of government with a greater range of responsibilities delivered to larger numbers of people. It became necessary, therefore, to find ways whereby the notion of popular sovereignty can made compatible with a workable decision-making process. This has given rise to a political system known as 'liberal democracy', although the scope for exercising independent judgement given to rulers under this system has resulted in the development of initiatives designed to bring government closer to the people. These include participatory democracy (where the general public is consulted on public policy decisions and may be empowered to share certain tasks of government with elected leaders) and direct democracy (in which devices such as referendum are used to involve the public in taking decisions on major policy issues).

see also...

Liberal democracy; Media; Participation; Referendum

Dependency

Dependency seeks to explain the unequal relationship that exists between first world countries over those in the third (or developing) world. It suggests that the overt political control formerly exercised by developed nations over their colonies (sometimes referred to as 'dependencies') has given way to a new form of dominance exerted over third world countries based upon the economic power of the first world. Factors such as the superior market position of first world countries and the reliance of the third world on foreign aid and development loans from the first world, form the basis for the economic imbalance between countries of the first and third world and from which the latter find escape hard.

Dependency suggests the existence of an economic form of colonialism which seeks to ensure that third world countries serve the economic interests of the industrially advanced nations by supplying raw materials required by the industries of the first world and then by serving as a market for the goods they produce. This tends to distort the pattern of economic development in such countries, which is typically concentrated on agriculture and the mining of minerals to the detriment of the development of domestic manufacturing industry. Dependency is buttressed by loans made available to third world countries by bodies such as the International Monetary Fund. The interest rates charged and the conditions stipulated by the lending body erode the sovereignty of the receiving country and may result in the pursuance of policies that are to the detriment of many of its inhabitants and place the country in a weak position from which to pursue economic development.

The economically subordinate position of third world countries is not, however, totally irreversible. Oil-exporting countries, for example, have been able to turn the tables on the first world when, acting through the Organisation of the Petroleum Exporting Countries (OPEC), they have initiated major changes in the price of oil by their ability to raise or cut production.

see also...

Colonialism; Sovereignty; Third world

Devolution

Devolution entails the transfer of power from a superior to an inferior political body. Typically central government cedes the ability to make law in specified areas to a regional or local unit of government but remains superior in the sense that it retains sovereignty and thus possesses the ability to take back the power that has been given away. This is unlike the situation in a federal system of government in which the powers given to sub-national units of government are held on a permanent basis in accordance with the provisions of a written constitution.

Devolution may enable national government and strong regional affiliations to be reconciled, thereby preserving national unity when threatened with intense 'home rule' sentiments. This is the case in Spain. In 1979, 17 regions (or 'autonomous communities') were set up, each with an assembly and a president. These bodies were able to nurture regional identity through the control they possessed over key public policy issues such as language.

In the United Kingdom devolution was catered for in a series of measures passed in 1998. The provisions affecting Scotland and Wales were designed to placate the demands for self-government (or 'home rule') put forward by nationalist parties (the Scottish National Party and *Plaid Cymru*). In Scotland a parliament was created with powers to make law over a wide range of domestic issues and with limited powers to raise some of its own finances.

In Wales, powers administered by the Welsh Office were transferred to an assembly of 60 persons. The assembly possesses no law-making or independent tax-raising powers and remains totally reliant on the block grant. This body thus democratised existing administrative arrangements rather than introducing a true form of devolution. Arrangements for Northern Ireland (embracing an assembly and power-sharing executive) were designed to end the period of direct rule from London (which had been instituted in 1972).

see also...

Consociationalism; Federal system of government; Sovereignty; Unitary system of government

Direct action

Direct action is a form of extra-parliamentary politics which seeks to advance a cause through some form of physical action. The tactics of direct action are varied, ranging from mainly non-violent methods such as civil disobedience, sit-ins, blockades and occupations to actions involving considerable use of force and violence associated with terrorist organisations (which may arise when those who conduct activities which a group opposes are the target of a physical sanction). The objectives sought by direct action are broad and include promoting local concerns, seeking to alter the direction of government policy or repudiating the political system.

Direct action is frequently practiced by social movements and pressure groups. These may seek to remedy social problems through their own efforts or they may seek to make the general public the focus of attempts to further their cause. This may involve educating the public to support the views of the group but it may entail the use of tactics designed to inconvenience or even intimidate the public in the expectation that public opinion will exert pressure on the government to change its policy.

Direct action occurs in all liberal democracies, although the importance attached to it as a means of securing change varies. In France, for example, direct action is frequently used as a method of first resort by groups wishing to alter government policy, whereas in the United Kingdom such methods have traditionally been used as a last resort, when other ways to influence the content of public policy have failed. The growing interdependence of nations (especially the growth of supranational bodies such as the European Union) may induce the wider use of direct action. In 2000, for example, the ability of direct action in France to force its government to reduce the tax on fuel resulted in the blockade of fuel distribution points in the United Kingdon by protesters with a similar objective.

see also...

Extra-parliamentary political activity; Liberal democracy; Political culture; Pressure group; Social movement; Terrorism

Elections

Elections are the mechanism whereby the views of the citizens of a particular country are translated into political actions. They serve a number of key roles. They facilitate popular sovereignty, providing citizens with ultimate political power. They enable citizens to participate in key political activities, such as selecting the personnel of government and determining the content of public policy. Elections are the mechanism through which accountability is secured. It is an essential feature of liberal democracy that sovereignty rests with the people living in each country. Governments must be accountable to the people for their actions. Those that lose the backing of public opinion can be replaced at the next round of elections. Elections also provide an essential link between the government and the governed by serving as a barometer of public opinion, ensuring that the holders of public office, and the policies which they pursue, are broadly in accord with the wishes of the general public.

A key role of elections in a liberal democratic political system election is to choose the country's rulers who then operate in accordance with the wishes of the public as expressed in an election. Election campaigns are therefore a prominent aspect of political participation in a liberal democratic political system. These campaigns may have a number of roles. They may reinforce a voter's existing loyalty to a political party or activate a party's existing supporters and ensure that they turn out and vote on election day: the identification by a party of its supporters is thus an important feature of campaigning. Election campaigns may also seek to convert members of the general public and thus gain new sources of electoral support for a party.

The importance of election campaigns is increased by partisan and class dealignment which increases the number of voters whose political allegiance is not pre-determined. Campaigns contribute towards shaping the choice of political party for the 'don't knows' and floating voters.

see also...

Accountability; Dealignment; Liberal democracy; Participation; Sovereignty

Elite

Elite theory is concerned with the distribution of power within society. In contrast to pluralism, elite theory suggests that power is not diffused (that is, widely spread throughout society) but, rather, is concentrated in the hands of a relatively small, organised minority of citizens who are able to enforce their will on the majority of citizens. This means that the many are governed by the few. This minority constitutes a political elite that exercises a dominant position in the policy making process. Elite theory suggests that elite domination occurs in any political system making all of them fundamentally undemocratic.

The composition of the political elite varies between societies. In pre-capitalist periods it commonly consisted of large landowners whose wealth and power was passed down from one generation to the next. In modern industrial societies elites consist of widely differing groups based upon factors such as social background, formal political office or technical or intellectual expertise. Marxists assert that elites consist of the economically dominant members of society whose wealth is the basis of their political power.

Elite theorists differ in their opinions concerning whether elitism and pluralist democracy are incompatible. Some suggest that competition between elites upholds the basic principle of pluralism. Others emphasise that the elites that compete for power are similar in terms of factors such as social background, attitudes and values, so that a similar group dominates the political system regardless of their political affiliation.

A leading elite theorist was Roberto Michels (1876–1936) whose 'iron law of oligarchy' was put forward in his work *Political Parties* (1915). He suggested that the need for organisations to possess bureaucracies in order to operate effectively meant that those at the top of the bureaucratic hierarchy were powerful and that the organisation itself was fundamentally undemocratic.

see also...

Authority; Marxism–Leninism; Pluralism; Political system; Power

Equality

Equality refers to the ideal of all citizens being equal. There are several forms this can take.

Initially, equality sought to remove the privileges enjoyed by certain groups within society so that all of its members were able to lead their lives without impediments being placed on them derived from factors such as birth, race, gender or religion. This is termed formal equality. This perception of a shared common humanity underpinned the extension of civic rights to all members of society. These included the rule of law and reforms such as the abolition of slavery and the removal of restrictions to voting thus providing for universal male and female enfranchisement.

Although formal equality removed the unfair disadvantages operating against some citizens, it did not tackle the underlying social or economic factors that might enable some members of society to achieve more than others. Other forms of equality have addressed this issue. Social equality is especially concerned with improving the status and self esteem of traditionally disadvantaged groups in society. Equality of opportunity has underpinned reforms materially to aid the poorer and weaker members of society. This can be achieved by some measure of redistribution of wealth or to measures (including equal opportunities and affirmative action programmes) designed to help disadvantaged groups (including women, racial minorities and physically handicapped persons) who have experienced discrimination in areas such as employment opportunities, pay and housing allocation.

Some socialists favour equality of outcome, which seeks a common level of attainment regardless of an individual's background, personal circumstances or the position they occupy in society. This may entail a levelling out process such as the abolition of wage differentials so that all persons were paid the same wage regardless of the job they performed.

see also...

Affirmative action; Citizenship; Civil rights; Feminism; Racism; Rule of law

European Union

The European Union (EU) is a supranational body seeking closer cooperation between the countries of Europe. The first step towards cooperation was the establishment in 1951 of the European Coal and Steel Community. This was followed in 1955 by the formation of the European Investment Fund. The Treaty of Rome (1957) established the European Economic Community (EEC) (popularly referred to as the Common Market) and Euratom (the European Atomic Energy Community). The EEC initially consisted of six countries (France, West Germany, Italy, the Netherlands, Belgium and Luxembourg). The United Kingdom, Ireland and Denmark joined in 1973, Greece in 1981, Spain and Portugal in 1986, and Austria, Finland and Sweden in 1995.

A number of subsequent key treaties have affected the development of the European Union. The Single European Act (1986) sought to remove obstacles to a frontier-free community by providing the legal framework to achieve a single market by 31 December 1992. This entailed the free movement of goods, services, capital and people between member states.

The Maastricht Treaty (1991) aimed to provide a legal basis for developments concerned with European political union and economic and monetary union and laid down the conditions for member countries joining a single currency. Moves towards common foreign and security policies and an extension of responsibilities in areas which included justice, home affairs and social policy were also proposed. Following ratification of this treaty in 1993, the term 'European Union' was employed, implying the creation of an organisation going beyond the original aims of the EEC. At the Brussels Summit of the European heads of government in 1998, the finance ministers of 11 countries agreed to implement the objectives of the Maastricht Treaty and create a single European currency, the euro. A single European currency ended the ability of individual governments to use interest rates to control the growth of their economies. Increased political union might stem from the creation of single currency.

see also...

Confederation; Federal system of government; Sovereignty; Sovereignty of parliament

Executive branch of government

The executive branch of government directs the affairs of a nation by taking and implementing policy decisions. Its work is performed by two distinct sets of people: paid, permanent officials, who often occupy the status of civil servants, and politicians, who exercise political control over a nation's affairs and are usually referred to as 'the government'. The American Constitution placed the executive branch in the hands of a president, and in the United Kingdom it consists of the prime minister, cabinet and junior ministers.

The executive branch of government is headed by a chief executive. This official exercises a pre-eminent political position. He or she appoints and dismisses subordinate members of the government, initiates proposals for government policy and oversees the administration and execution of policy and the overall conduct of the government, thereby giving coherence to its work. The chief executive mobilises support for the policies of the government and may be required to act in times of crisis since firm leadership is usually best provided by a single person.

There are, however, limits to the power of chief executives. These may derive from the operations of presidential and parliamentary forms of government. American presidents may have difficulties in getting their proposals through congress especially when it is controlled by a rival political party and the strength of chief executives in parliamentary forms of government is influenced by factors such as the size of their parliamentary majority and the unity of their parliamentary party. The political climate within which chief executives operate may also affect their power. In America, for example, events such as the Vietnam War (which was associated with presidential initiative) and the enforced resignation of President Nixon in 1974 made the public suspicious of presidents who wished to exercise dynamic leadership.

see also...

Bureaucracy; Cabinet; Coalition government; Legislative branch of government; Political system; Power; Presidential system of government; Separation of powers

Extra-parliamentary political activity

Extra-parliamentary political activity entails actions undertaken by groups of citizens who seek to influence a state's decision-making process by a wide range of methods, including demonstrations, industrial disputes, civil disobedience, direct action, riots and terrorism. These methods offer an alternative mean of political action to that provided by conventional political activity.

The ability to engage in extra-parliamentary political activity is an important feature of all liberal democratic political systems and it possesses a number of advantages to aid their operations. These include enabling citizens to involve themselves in the government of their country beyond periodic voting in elections and permitting them to exert influence over specific items of policy that are of concern to them. Extra-parliamentary politics may succeed in raising minority interests and also guard against political apathy resulting from a tendency to defer all political decisions to a country's leaders which could result in a totalitarian system of government.

There are, however, problems associated with extra-parliamentary politics. Violence and public disorder may arise, perhaps based upon a desire by a group to achieve political aims through intimidation or coercion. In these cases, a government may be required to intervene in order to prevent citizens or their property being subject to the threat or actuality of violence. Conventional politics conducted through the ballot box may be viewed as an irrelevant form of activity if other means are widely practiced and are seen to be successful and such actions may also undermine a government's capacity for governing if it is forced to follow a course of action advocated by groups using extra-parliamentary methods. A government in this situation may appear weak which may create a desire for the imposition of 'strong' government.

see also...

Agenda setting; Direct action; Elections; Liberal democracy; Participation; Political culture; Pressure group; Social movement; Totalitarian

Faction

The term faction denotes the existence of a minority group within a larger body that takes issue with the majority over the leadership of that body or the policies it advocates. It consists of a group with formal organisation and a relatively stable membership and is effectively a 'party within a party'. The Italian Christian Democrats are sometimes described as a coalition of several factions and the Japanese Liberal Democratic Party is similarly composed of a wide range of factions.

Factions need to be distinguished from tendencies. These also exist within a political party and consist of people who share common opinions. Unlike factions, however, they lack formal organisation. During Margaret Thatcher's period of office as prime minister in the United Kingdom (1979–1990) the 'Wets' were a tendency within the Conservative Party opposed to many of her policies. Towards the end of the 1990s a further tendency emerged within that party, the Eurosceptics. These were opposed to any further moves towards the pooling of sovereignty and political integration within the European Union and in particular opposed the goal of the 1991 Maastricht Treaty of economic and monetary union. In 1995 Eurosceptics supported the leadership challenge mounted by John Redwood to the then Conservative party leader and prime minister, John Major.

In the United States the term faction is closer in meaning to its eighteenth century definition of 'party'. Key provisions contained in the American Constitution including the separation of powers and the system of checks and balances were devised to prevent a majority faction seizing control of the government and riding roughshod over minority interests. James Madison (1751–1836) exerted considerable influence over these provision of the Constitution, believing that factions were derived from the unequal distribution of wealth.

see also...

European Union; Political party; Separation of powers; Sovereignty

Fascism

Fascism is a political ideology on the right of the political spectrum which, although lacking a coherent body of beliefs, possesses certain common features. These include opposition to communism, Marxism and liberalism (especially individualism which they advocate should occupy a subordinate position to the national community). Fascism also opposes the operations of liberal democracy that it seeks to replace with a totalitarian political system in which there is only one party and, ideally, the complete identity of this party with the state. One consequence of this is that civil and political liberties are absent in fascist states.

Fascist parties utilise action and violence as key political tactics especially when seeking to secure power and they stress the importance of firm leadership to solve a nation's problems. Prominent leaders fascist movements such as Adolf Hitler (1889–1945) in Germany, Benito Mussolini (1883–1945) in Italy, Francisco Franco (1892–1975) in Spain, and Antonio de Oliveira Salazar (1889–1970) in Portugal made great use of their personal charisma to secure loyalty from those who followed them. Fascist movements also emphasise the importance of nation and race whose consequences included a desire for territorial expansion and the practice of racism and genocide.

Fascist movements appeal to people of all social classes by using populist rhetoric to secure support. Successful fascist parties attract the lower middle classes when these feel threatened by social and economic changes occurring in a particular country. There was, however, wide variation in the ideas and policies put forward by individual fascist parties whose leaders cultivated support by opportunistically exploiting popular concerns, fears or prejudices. This meant that the success achieved by fascist parties was significantly influenced by events that were unique to particular countries.

see also...

Civil rights; Corporatism; Ideology; Liberalism; Marxism–Leninism; Nationalism; Political spectrum; Populism; Totalitarian

Federal system of government

A federal system of government describes a political structure that is characterised by the division of power between the national (sometimes referred to as 'federal') government and the constituent states. Countries that have such a system includes Germany and America. The division of responsibilities is provided for in a single source, usually a written constitution, that allocates specific functions to each sphere of government. Each enjoys autonomy in its own area of jurisdiction which means that one may not intrude into the operations of the other. There may also be functions that are exercised jointly by both tiers of government.

Federalism was historically viewed as a safeguard against the overbearing power of a strong, central government. In large countries it breaks down the remoteness that might otherwise occur if government were provided by a distant national authority and thus brings government closer to the people. Federalism empowers localities to run most aspects of their affairs in accordance with the wishes of the people who reside there with restricted 'interference' by a national government. It may thus contribute towards retaining the existence of states threatened by separatist tendencies.

There are, however, difficulties associated with federalism. Diverse standards of service provision within a single country are not necessarily desirable and a minority may be given the means to frustrate the will of the majority. The progress of civil rights in America was impeded by the governments of the southern states which opposed this legislation.

In many federal countries there has been a tendency for the power of national governments to be enhanced at the expense of states whose independence is also restricted by their reliance on revenue provided by national government and the imposition of national requirements governing service provision.

see also...

Confederation; Constitution; Sovereignty; Unitary system of government

Feminism

Feminism refers to a wide range of theories that assert that the power relationship between the sexes is unequal viewing this problem as a social construction rather than a natural situation arising from biological differences between male and female. The modern feminist movement derived from North America in the 1960s.

There are a number of strands to feminist thought. Liberal feminism seeks to combat discrimination experienced by women in the public sphere and seeks equality of treatment. Measures to secure formal equality embodied in equal rights legislation (such as the United Kingdom's 1970 Equal Pay Act and 1975 Sex Discrimination Act) derive from this perspective.

Radical feminism seeks the liberation of women. This focuses not on inequality but, rather, on the system of sexual oppression, termed 'patriarchy' (or 'rule by men'). Radical feminists believe that patriarchy is the key power relationship in society and is reproduced in each generation by the family. They believe that sexual equality requires a revolution in cultural and social values and cannot be attained by providing additional legal rights for women within the existing social structure. Marxist feminism attributes the oppression of women to the operations of capitalism that gives rise to economic dependency, viewed as the basis of women's oppression. They assert that only in a communist society would this situation be remedied. Socialist feminism concentrates on the way in which the twin forces of patriachy and class oppression interact in a capitalist society and place women in a socially subordinate position. Unlike radical feminists, however, they do not view the interests of men and women as being permanently opposed. Postmodernist feminism rejects the certainty and objectivity that underlaid the Marxist view of class interests. They do not see all women as being subject to the same processes and believed that different groups encounter different experiences.

see also...

Equality; Extra-parliamentary political activity; Representation; Social movement

First-past-the-post system of voting

The first-past-the-post voting system requires one candidate to secure more votes than the person who comes second in order to be elected to a public office. But there is no requirement that the winning candidate should secure an overall majority of the votes cast in that election. This method is used in countries including the United Kingdom and America.

The first-past-the-post electoral system is easy to understand. There are, however, a number of disadvantages associated with it. It distorts public opinion by failing to ensure that the wishes of the electorate are arithmetically reflected in the composition of legislatures and in particular discriminates against minority parties by failing to translate their national vote into seats in this body. The first-past-the-post system is also capable of producing extreme political changes. Major political parties can be virtually wiped out overnight, as occurred in the 1993 Canadian general election when the ruling Conservative Party was reduced from 157 seats to two in the House of Commons.

The problems associated with the first-past-the-post system of voting have encouraged the development of variants of this system. These include the second ballot and the alternative vote, both of which require a candidate to obtain an overall majority of votes cast (that is, 50%+1) in order to secure election. If no candidate obtains this figure, under the second ballot a second-round election is held when, in order to win, a candidate must get the endorsement of a majority of the electors who vote. With the alternative vote, voters number candidates in order of preference. If no candidate possesses an overall majority, the candidate with least first-preference votes is eliminated and these are redistributed to the candidate placed second on that candidate's ballot paper. This process is repeated until a candidate has an overall majority composed of his or her first-preference votes coupled with the redistributed votes of eliminated candidates.

see also...

Adversarial politics; Legislative branch of government; Proportional representation

Freedom

Freedom suggests that individuals are able to live their lives as they see fit with no impediments being placed on their actions. However, this assertion would find little support outside anarchist thought: other ideologies suggest that some form of regulation needs to be applied since unrestrained freedom would enable some members of society to harm others. A key issue affecting freedom, therefore, is the relationship between the individual and the state, and under what circumstances it is acceptable for the state to undertake interventions that intrude on some or all of its members.

Liberal thought saw a close distinction between freedom and rights. Freedom was especially associated with civil liberties and was defined in a negative sense whereby individuals were deemed free to undertake actions unless the interests of others required that constraints be placed upon them. Freedom was equated with privacy and minimal state activity since this would limit an individual's freedom of action.

The concept of freedom was later developed in liberal thought into that of positive freedom which viewed a more vigorous form of state activity as essential to enable individuals to exercise freedom that was defined in terms of self-fulfilment. Industrial capitalism had created conditions whereby large numbers of individuals lived in poverty. Deprived individuals needed state action (typically in the form of a welfare state and intervention in the management of the economy) to create conditions in which they regained autonomy over the conduct of their lives.

In the late twentieth century neo-liberals focused on an economic definition of freedom that was equated with the advocacy of free market capitalism and the reduction of state interference in social and economic affairs. It was asserted that state intervention had eroded freedom by constraining consumer choice and by transforming recipients of state aid into a position of dependency.

see also...

Anarchism; Capitalism; Individualism; Liberalism; New right; Political toleration; Privacy

Freedom of information

Freedom of information requires public bodies or officials to make available to citizens a wide range of public documents. Public access was first granted in Sweden in 1766 but in other countries has been a twentieth-century development. Freedom of information legislation exists in America and Germany where it is a considerable aid to investigative journalism. In America the 1966 and 1974 Freedom of Information Acts provided citizens and interest groups with the right to inspect most federal records. Although access to some information may be denied an appeal to the courts may secure the production of the desired information. New Zealand also has an Official Information Act which permits public access to a wide range of information.

The 'right to know' is viewed as an important civil right in liberal democratic countries, enabling citizens to hold their governments to account for the actions they have taken. There are, however, limits placed on the public's ability to have access to official material. Typically, this is constrained by the desire to prevent unwarranted intrusion into an individual's privacy and also to safeguard national security. Legislation exists in a number of liberal democracies to restrict the release of official information that may be used to prevent the media from publishing material deemed contrary to state interests. This includes Ireland's 1939 Offences Against the State Act and the United Kingdom's 1989 Official Secrets Act.

Legislation to prevent the release of information has sometimes posed dilemmas for civil servants who have believed that politicians confuse state interests with their own political considerations and seek to use the former grounds to suppress information that might have damaging political consequences. This has given rise to the phenomenon of 'whistleblowing' that involves a civil servant leaking information to the media when he or she believes the public's right to know superseded the concern of a government to keep this material secret.

see also...

Accountability; Liberal democracy; Media; Privacy

Globalisation

Globalisation refers to the increasing integration of nations that affects a wide range of issues including cultural and political affairs (especially the spread of liberal democratic political values). It has arisen as the result of a number of developments. One of these is communications technology such as the internet and satellite television which has made it difficult for governments to censure the spread of ideas and has also facilitated the organisation of protest on an international scale (such as the worldwide anti-capitalist movement). A particularly important aspect of globalisation is the increasing integration of world economies arising from the ease with which goods and capital can be transferred across national boundaries.

The global economy emphasises the interrelationships of the economies of nation states, emphasising that the success or failure of the economy of one nation, or block of nations, has a major impact throughout the world. This may result in a 'governance gap' whereby nation states are powerless to control processes that occur at a global level.

The economic aspect of globalisation was illustrated by events towards the end of 1998. The Russian currency (the rouble) lost its value against key world currencies such as the dollar and pound leading to its government devaluing the currency and postponing debt repayments. These actions, however, provoked economic difficulties that spread far beyond Russia. They resulted in a flight of capital; since western investors (who stood to lose huge sums of money from unpaid loans in Russia) sold shares worldwide and turn to safer forms of investment. This selling had an immediate consequence for the economic policies pursued by individual Latin American and Asian nations, who were forced to consider devaluation of their currencies or making large rises in interest rates. The economic difficulties of Latin American countries had a subsequent effect in America and Europe, especially in countries (such as Spain) whose banks had large investments in that part of the world.

see also...

Media; Nationalism; Social movement; Sovereignty

Head of state

A head of state is a public official viewed as the leading citizen of his or her country. This office possesses a higher degree of authority than that enjoyed by governments since it is viewed as standing above party politics. The office of head of state is separate from that of chief executive (although in presidential forms of government it is exercised by the same person, the president).

There is considerable variety within liberal democracies concerning the selection of a head of state. Britain, Holland, Belgium and the Scandinavian countries have constitutional monarchs as heads of state whose position is derived from birth. In other countries the head of state is subject to some form of election. Such countries are termed republics. This may involve a process of direct election (as is the case in Ireland) or indirect election (in Italy and Germany).

Heads of state fulfil a number of functions. They provide a rallying point for national unity and usually appoint chief executives and approve legislation. In most cases these are formal endorsements of decisions that have already been made. But the participation of the head of state neutralises the political dimension of the activity. The involvement of a head of state in selecting a chief executive, for example, suggests that this official serves the whole nation and not merely the political interests that person represents. Heads of state usually possess the power to intervene in the conduct of political affairs to ensure its smooth conduct by being able to dismiss the government or dissolve the legislature.

An elected head of state may seek to exercise a major role in the political life of a country. Mary Robinson (born 1944) used her tenure as President of Ireland (1990–1997) to promote radical policies to advance the position of the needy and remedy the perception of women as second class citizens.

see also...

Executive branch of government; Liberal democracy; Parliamentary system of government; Presidential system of government

Human rights

Human rights consist of basic entitlements that should be available to all human beings living in any society. Unlike civil rights, (specific to individual countries) human rights are universal in application.

Human rights developed from the tradition of natural rights which sought to establish boundaries to protect an individual being interfered with by other citizens or by the government and were thus intimately associated with the objective of liberalism that government should be limited in its actions, which was an important aspect of liberal thought. These rights were thus essentially negative, seeking to impose restraints on the action that others might wish to undertake. The English political philosopher, John Locke (1632–1704), suggested that human rights embraced 'life, liberty and property' while the American statesman Thomas Jefferson (1743–1826) indicated that they included 'life, liberty and the pursuit of happiness'. These were rights to which all persons were entitled simply as a consequence of being a human being and which no government could take away since to do so would constitute a denial of their humanity.

A recent declaration of human rights is to be found in the European Convention for the Protection of Human Rights and Fundamental Freedoms (1950). This asserts the right to life, liberty, security, the right to respect private and family life (including the right to marry and found a family), the right to a fair trial, the right to freedom of thought, conscience, religion, expression and assembly and prohibits torture, inhuman and degrading treatment, slavery and enforced labour, all forms of discrimination and declares that there should be no punishment without law. Protocols to this declaration assert the right to peaceful participation in processions and to education.

Human rights may be defended by international bodies (such as the European Court of Human Rights) and be incorporated into the domestic law of individual countries.

see also...

Civil rights; Constitution; Judicial branch of government; Judicial review; Liberalism; Marxism–Leninism; Privacy

Ideology

Ideology is commonly defined as the principles that motivate political parties, in particular providing a vision of the society they wish to create. Ideology thus serves as a unifying force between party leaders and supporters: all are spiritually united in the promotion of a common cause.

Ideology is not, however, always the guiding force in party politics. American political parties appear far less ideological than their western European counterparts. Even in these countries, parties may abandon ideology in favour of pragmatism (that is, responding to events as they occur without referring to any preconceived ideology).

There is a danger that politicians are perceived as seeking office for the power that it gives them as individuals where ideology is not prominent as a driving force motivating a political party. The absence of pronounced ideology may also result in a situation in which electors find it difficult to differentiate between the political parties.
Marxists adopt a more precise definition of ideology. Here it refers to a coherent set of ideas, beliefs and values through which an individual can make sense of the social world they inhabit. This ought to derive from a person's social class. However, Marxists contend that liberal democracies are dominated by the ideology of the ruling class (or bourgeoisie) that secures the acquiesence of the working class (proletariat) to exploitation and social inequality. The dominance accorded to bourgeois ideas in such societies (arising from the control they exert over agencies such as the education system and the media) results in the proletariat suffering from what Friedrich Engels (1820–95) referred to as a 'false consciousness' whereby they fail to appreciate the fact that they are exploited and thus consent to the operations of the existing social system which is thus accorded legitimacy by this intellectual form of control.

see also...

Consensus politics; Elections; Legitimacy; Marxism–Leninism; Political spectrum; Social democracy; Socialism

Incrementalism

Incrementalism refers to a view of policy making that suggests that those who make decisions merely seek to make small adjustments to existing policy rather than embark upon a lengthy process involving a comprehensive evaluation of all the options open to them.

This approach was particularly associated with the American, Charles Lindblom, whose initial contribution was contained in an article, entitled 'The Science of "Muddling Through"', published in 1959. This suggested that policy making was a spasmodic activity whereby the actions of policy makers did not conform to a coherent science, guided by the pursuit of objectives. Instead their intervention was of a reactive nature, responding to issues (which were mainly of a short term nature) in an *ad hoc* fashion. Additionally, policy making was alleged to be conservative in that policy makers did not substantially depart from the status quo. This meant that the content of new policies was greatly influenced by existing ones and radical innovations were not attempted. Finally, policy making was said to be remedial in the sense that it was not concerned with a 'once and for all' solution to a problem that had been identified. Rather, its scope was limited to managing problems as and when they arose.

This approach to policy making was primarily viewed as descriptive rather than prescriptive. That is, it was concerned with explaining what actually happened as opposed to ideally how decisions would be made. Its advantages included taking into account the political environment within which public policy was fashioned. One key explanation offered by Lindblom for incrementalism was partisan mutual adjustment. This meant that policy makers were engaged in a perpetual game of 'give and take' with each other for reasons that included competition for scarce resources. This process of negotiation resulted in policy makers having to dilute their more radical proposals in order to secure the support of others for more modest programmes.

see also...

Agenda setting; Bureaucracy

Individualism

Individualism places the interests of individual citizens at the forefront of its concerns and is viewed as the opposite of collectivism. As a political doctrine it suggests that the sphere of government should be limited so as not to encroach unduly on the ability of individuals to pursue their own interests and thereby achieve self fulfilment. As an economic principle, individualism opposes government intervention in the workings of the economy in preference to support for the free market and laissez faire capitalism (which saw no place for government imposing restrictions affecting matters such as wages and conditions of work).

Individualism was historically linked to liberalism whose classical notion of limited government (derived from natural rights) held that individuals should be as free as possible from state interference since this would deprive them of their ability to exercise responsibility for the conduct of their lives. It could, however, be justified in order to prevent actions by some which would impede the ability of others to advance their interests. This belief would, for example, justify legislation against monopolists since these prejudiced the position of individual entrepreneurs. State involvement in social policy (especially to protect the poorer and weaker members of society) was rejected by liberals for much of the nineteenth century, by the same token, on the grounds that individuals should be responsible for their own welfare.

Individualism was thus historically viewed as the opposite of collectivism. However, some strands of liberal thought have suggested their compatibility by arguing that individual enterprise is hindered by circumstances such as the operations of the economy that are not of the individual's own making. State action directed at those who are placed in such circumstances can thus be justified in the belief that it would remove impediments preventing people from being able to assert control over their own destinies.

see also...

Collectivism; Conservatism; Freedom; Human rights; Liberalism; New right

Judicial branch of government

The judicial branch of government is composed of judges whose role is to adjudicate a dispute between two parties. These may be private citizens who are in dispute with each other (which is termed a civil case) or the state may be involved in a case that comes before the courts. This may arise either when a person is charged with a criminal offence or when a citizen is in dispute with the state which is the concern of administrative law. In some countries (such as France) a separate system of administrative courts exists, while in others (such as the United Kingdom) cases of this nature are heard in the regular courts. The judiciary also performs the function of judicial review and the requirement of judges not merely to enforce the law but also to interpret it may enable them effectively to act as law makers (a situation which is termed 'judicial activism').

No two liberal democratic countries have an identical judicial system. Differences exist concerning the conduct of trials. The adversarial system is used in Britain and America, the essence of which is that two parties seek to prove their case by conflicting the arguments put forward by their opponents. Alternatively, the inquisitorial system is used in a number of European countries, including France. Here the gathering of evidence is the responsibility of a magistrate or judge and the main function of the trial is to resolve issues uncovered in the earlier investigation.

The ability of the judiciary to act independently from the other two branches of government is an important aspect of liberal democratic political systems and is upheld through the principle of security of tenure. Judges are affected by formal and informal controls. In particular they may be influenced by public opinion and seek to ensure that their judgements accord with this. It has been argued that the American Supreme Court watches the election returns.

see also...

Constitution; Executive branch of government; Judicial review; Legislative branch of government; Liberal democracy; Separation of powers

Judicial review

Judicial review is a process whereby the judiciary is able to scrutinise the actions undertaken by the executive and legislative branches of government and other subordinate units of government in order to ensure that provisions contained in codified constitutions are upheld. If the courts decide that the actions placed before it for examination are in breach of the constitution they may be declared 'unconstitutional'. This has the effect of overturning them.

In America, judicial review is performed by the Supreme Court and France, the *Conseil Constitutionnel* is responsible for ensuring that the constitution is adhered to and, in Germany, the federal constitutional court exercises this function.

Codified constitutions frequently contain statements of principle that embody its spirit and set the tone for subsequent judicial interpretation. In this manner the constitution may validly be applied to situations and events that were not envisaged when the original document was written, thereby enabling it to be kept up to date without having to undergo a complex process of amendment. In performing this task judges may draw solely on their legal expertise or they may, as in the case in Germany, consider submissions from interested parties before reaching a judgement. One difficulty with judicial review, however, is that it may result in the courts failing to limit the scope of executive power meaningfully or force it to subscribe to any basic standard of behaviour.

Countries such as the United Kingdom which have uncodified constitutions have a different process of judicial review. This is because the law passed by the legislature is itself a source of the constitution. In these countries the scope of judicial review is more limited, being confined to an assessment or whether the provisions contained in law passed by the legislature have been strictly observed by the executive branch of government or subordinate units such as local government.

see also...

Constitution; Judicial branch of government; Legislative branch of government

Legislative branch of government

The legislative branch of government performs law-making functions. In the United Kingdom the legislature is referred to as parliament and in America as congress. Elected legislatures symbolise representative government, the institution which links the government and the governed.

Making the law (or amending or repealing it) is a key function of legislatures and a specific aspect of this role is approving the budget and granting authority for the collection of taxes. This task has been affected by the tendency for legislatures to respond to the initiatives of the executive branch in both presidential and parliamentary systems of government. Additionally, they debate policy and other issues of public importance. Such debates are published in official journals and are publicised by the media thus providing a source of information for the general public.

Legislatures scrutinise the actions undertaken by the executive branch of government and may thus exert influence over its conduct. In parliamentary systems of government scrutiny is linked to the concept of ministerial responsibility. Scrutiny may include approving the nomination of individual members of the government put forward by the chief executive and may also extend to the operations of the bureaucracy. This function (which in America is termed 'oversight') entails ensuring that an agency is meeting the goals specified for it, that the public money provided for it is being spent for the purposes for which it was intended or that an operation is conducted in accordance with any restrictions initially placed on it by the legislature.

Legislatures may perform judicial functions, including the ability to regulate the conduct of their members. They are solely responsible for initiating and determining constitutional change in countries with flexible constitutions.

see also...

Accountability; Bureaucracy; Constitution; Executive branch of government; Media; Ministerial responsibility; Parliamentary system of government; Presidential system of government; Representation; Separation of powers

Legitimacy

Legitimacy entails popular acceptance of the exercise of power within a political system. It is closely linked to the concept of authority, being commonly applied to political systems whereas authority is generally applied to specific public officials. Legitimacy is a quality that confers acceptance of the actions undertaken by the government from those it governs. Those who are subject to such rules may not necessarily approve of them but legitimacy involves an acceptance that the government has the right to make decisions and that the public has a duty to obey them.

In liberal democratic political systems, legitimacy is founded on the notion of popular consent. Governments derive their position from elections. This is a process in which all citizens are entitled to participate and are required to in countries where voting is compulsory. The support obtained at an election is the basis of a government's claim on the obedience of its citizens to the actions that they subsequently undertake provided that they act in accordance within the established rules of political conduct. Marxists, however, emphasise that legitimacy entails public acceptance of the distribution of power within society. This is not derived from genuine popular approval but, rather, is the product of ideological control exerted in the interests of the ruling class over the masses which is designed to secure their acceptance of political, social and economic inequality.

Legitimacy, whether it derives from manipulation or genuine popular approval, is important in establishing stable government able to draw on the obedience of its citizens. This may, however, be undermined by political, social or economic factors such as repeated failures by governments to act in accordance with the wishes of their citizens or by perceptions that those who occupy political office seek to use their position to bring them personal benefits. Factors such as these may result in what is termed a 'legitimation crisis' in which citizens question the right of the government to act.

see also...

Authority; Elections; Ideology; Liberal democracy; Marxism–Leninism; Participation; Political system; Power; Sleaze

Liberal democracy

Liberal democracy is a political system with two fundamental characteristics. Government is 'liberal' in terms of the core values which underpin this system, and 'democratic' concerning the political arrangements that exist within it.

The core values associated with liberal democratic political systems accord to the traditional liberal belief in limited government and are designed to ensure that a broad measure of civil and human rights exists. These may be guaranteed by devices that include a constitution, a bill of rights, the separation of powers, a system of checks and balances and, crucially, the rule of law.

A democratic political system is one whose actions reflect the will of the people (or at least the majority of them). Popular consent in liberal democratic political systems is secured through representation: liberal (or, as it is sometimes referred to, representative) democracy entails a small group of people taking political decisions on behalf of all the citizens who live in a particular country. Those who exercise this responsibility do so with the consent of the citizens and govern in their name. However, their right to take decisions depends on popular approval and may be withdrawn should they lose the support of the population to whom they are accountable for their actions. In these cases citizens reclaim the political power they have ceded and reallocate the responsibility for government elsewhere. Elections that provide a genuine opportunity to exert popular choice over the actions and personnel of government are thus an essential aspect of liberal democracies. This requires all adults having the right to vote, the regular holding of elections and political parties being able openly to compete for power.

Liberal democratic political systems are particularly associated with the capitalist economies of first world countries.

see also...

Accountability; Civil rights; Democracy; Elections; Human rights; Legitimacy; Liberalism; Marxism–Leninism; Political toleration; Representation; Rule of law; Separation of powers

Liberalism

Modern liberalism emerged from the fight for religious freedom waged in late sixteenth- and seventeenth-century western Europe. The close link that existed between church and state ensured that the objective of religious freedom was associated with political dissent. Liberal theorists argued that the social order was a compact (or contract) voluntarily entered into by those who were party to it rather than being a structure handed down by God. Social contract theory was developed by liberal theorists such as Thomas Hobbes (1588–1679) and John Locke (1632–1704). The belief that government emerged as the result of rational choice made by those who subsequently accorded their consent to its operations ensured that the rights of the individual were prominent concerns of liberal philosophers. The people were viewed as the ultimate source of political power and government was legitimate only while it operated with their consent.

As a political doctrine, liberalism emphasised individualism and asserted that human beings should exercise the maximum possible freedom consistent with others being able to enjoy similar liberty. They sought to advance this belief through their support for limited government and their opposition to the intervention of the state in the everyday lives of its citizens, arguing that this would dehumanise individuals since they were not required to take responsibility for their own welfare but instead became reliant on others whom they could blame if personal misfortunes befell them. As an economic doctrine, liberalism was traditionally associated with the free market, laissez faire capitalism and free trade.

The perception that social problems such as unemployment and poverty were dependent on factors such as the workings of the economy over which the individual had no control, resulted in significant changes to liberal ideology. In many countries liberals advocated state intervention in welfare provision and economic management. Traditional liberal principles, subsequently influenced the new right in the 1980s.

see also...

Ideology; Individualism; Liberal democracy; New right; Realignment

Lobbying

Lobbying describes communication between someone other than a citizen acting on his or own behalf and a government policy maker with the intention of influencing the latter's decisions.

Lobbying is big business in America: in 1998 corporate (that is, business and commercial interests) there spent approximately £700 million a year to field 14,000 officially registered lobbyists in Washington, DC. This amounted to 27 lobbyists for each member of congress. In comparison the British lobbying industry had earnings of around £70 million a year.

Lobbying was traditionally an activity directed at the legislative branch of government, but has subsequently extended to the executive branch where politicians and bureaucrats are made the subject of this activity. Much lobbying is carried out by pressure groups. Some employ full-time lobbyists to promote their interests while others hire lobbyists on a temporary basis when they wish to advance, or secure the defeat of, legislation which is relevant to their interests. The influence they are able to exert over policy makers is derived from their being regarded as an important source of information. In the United Kingdom, parliamentary lobbyists (or parliamentary consultants) provide political advice and analysis that may be sought by commercial companies or by other governmental organisations. The most influential lobbyists are those who have established regular contacts in the legislative or executive branches of government and in this sense they act as a conduit to power.

Lobbying consists of a variety of activities, ranging from personal approaches to policy makers to bribery. It is subject to varied forms of regulation. In America, the 1946 Federal Regulation of Lobbying Act required paid lobbyists, whose main purpose is to influence or defeat legislation, to register and state their policy goals and in Canada, the 1988 Lobbyists Registration Act required them to register.

see also...

Legislative branch of government; Pressure group

Local government

Local government has responsibility for providing a range of services to people living in part of a country. The scope of their activities and extent of their autonomy is widely varied. In many western European and Scandinavian countries local government is created by constitutional enactment and in America is provided for in state constitutions. In countries including France, Italy, Sweden and Denmark, local government has 'general competence', that is the ability to perform any function unless expressly forbidden to do so by law. In the United Kingdom and Ireland, however, local government has no constitutional status. Its existence is derived from legislation and it may only perform those functions that are expressly allocated to it by law passed by parliament. This situation vastly curtails the autonomy exercised by local authorities in these two countries, although in the United Kingdom discretionary powers provide some degree of operational and innovatory freedom.

Local government plays a number of important roles in liberal democratic political systems. It increases the extent of political participation by enabling citizens to vote in local elections or to put themselves forward for service as members of local authorities. Local government may act as a pressure group, putting forward local needs to other tiers of government. It is also an efficient mechanism to provide public services by enabling local concerns to be addressed. The elected dimension of local government is the key to its responsiveness to local issues and problems.

In many countries local government is a training ground for politicians who later occupy high national office. It may also link local people with national leaders. This is especially so in France where national politicians sometimes hold elected office in local government thus providing them with powerful localised bases of support.

see also...

Accountability; Constitution; Elections; Extra-parliamentary political activity; Federal system of government; Liberal democracy; Participation; Pressure group

Mandate

A mandate confers authority on a political party, having obtained an election victory, to govern in accordance with the contents of its election manifesto. Its right to do this has been legitimised by the process of popular election.

The mandate is influential in some liberal democracies such as the United Kingdom. It ensures that a political party declares the policies it intends to carry out if it wins an election. Parties are not thus unknown quantities: electors vote in an informed manner, their choice being determined by policy statements issued during an election contest. Conversely, the mandate implies that parties that embark on a significant course of action not placed before the electorate previously should seek such popular approval rather than acting without it. In other countries, the mandate may be of less importance. In America, for example, voters are heavily influenced by the record of incumbent candidates (that is, those who are seeking re-election to the office they currently occupy). There is a tendency to look back and cast votes in accordance with a candidate's past record rather than seeking to evaluate the merits of proposed future actions.

There are, however, weaknesses with the mandate. Issues emerge, unforeseen when the manifesto was prepared, that have to be responded to even though the public lacks the opportunity to express its views on them. Instead, it must be accepted that once installed in office, governments need to exercise a certain amount of discretion to respond to pressing problems when they arise. This capacity to act without consulting the general public is referred to as trusteeship. A further problem is that a party cannot claim the right to carry out its promises on the grounds that the public expressed support for all of them. Electors are unable to pick and choose from a manifesto those policies they like and those they disapprove of. Additionally, a party or its candidates may secure support for negative rather than positive reasons. This makes it difficult to claim they have a mandate for their policies.

see also...

Authority; Elections; Legitimacy; Political party

Marxism–Leninism

Marxism–Leninism combines the ideas of Karl Marx (1818–83) and Vladimir Ilych Lenin (1870–1924). Marx asserted that actions and human institutions were economically determined and that the class struggle was the key instrument of historical change. Lenin was especially concerned with the organisation of a post-capitalist society.

Marx held that industrialised societies were controlled by an economically dominant class, the bourgeoisie. Their wealth was the underpinning for their political power in which the state was used as an instrument to dominate and exploit the working class (or proletariat). Although those who owned and controlled capital were not necessarily the same as those who exercised political power, the economic interests and cultural values of the former determined the actions undertaken by the latter.

Marx stressed that social classes were in an inevitable state of competition with each other and that the exploitive nature of capitalism made a proletarian or working-class revolution inevitable. Exploitation would result in increased class consciousness. This would develop into class conflict, resulting in a revolution involving the overthrow of the ruling class and the emergence of a new society based on what he termed 'the dictatorship of the proletariat'. The new socialist society would be characterised by the abolition of private property ownership which was viewed as the basis of the inequalities of the class system.

Marx said little concerning how a socialist society should be organised. This was a major concern of Lenin's. He argued that it was the role of the Communist Party to act as the vanguard (that is, leader) of the proletariat which would direct the revolution and control society while true socialism was being constructed. This meant that a one party state operated in countries controlled by Marxist–Leninist ideology.

see also...

Authority; Capitalism; Communism; Elite; Ideology; Pluralism; Power; Socialism; State; Totalitarian

Media

The media are the means of communication including newspapers, television and newer developments such as the internet. Traditionally, in liberal democratic political systems, its operations were disconnected so that ownership of the print media was divorced from other major forms of communication such as radio and television. However, this barrier has been eroded by the growth of cross-media ownership which has given rise to a number of powerful media bosses such as Rupert Murdoch, with interests in a wide range of outlets.

The media serve a number of functions. They act as a source of information concerning domestic and international events and also act as a watchdog scrutinising the activities performed by governments. The term 'fourth estate' is often used to describe the function performed by the media as guardians of a country's constitution and its liberal democratic system of politics.

While it is generally accepted that the media are important to the functioning of liberal democracy, their operations are frequently subject to adverse comment. A major criticism is that they may display political bias in their reporting of events and seek to influence voting behaviour at election times.

There are various views concerning this. The reinforcement theory suggests that the power of the media over politics is limited since most members of the general public have preconceived political opinions. They will either read, listen or view material that is consistent with these existing ideas and ignore contrary ideas should they be expressed. A contrary opinion suggests that many people are unaware of the political biases of the media to which they are subject and may thus be influenced by the manner in which they portray events, especially when such exposure takes place over a long period of time. Those without established political views or loyalties (who are described as 'don't knows' in opinion polls) may be most susceptible to media influence.

see also...

Agenda setting; Legislative branch of government; Privacy; Public opinion polls

Ministerial responsibility

Ministerial responsibility refers to the relationship between members of the executive branch of government and the legislature. There are two forms of ministerial responsibility – collective and individual.

An important feature of parliamentary political structures is collective ministerial responsibility. This asserts the supremacy of the legislature by insisting that a government that loses the confidence of that body must resign.

The mechanics of collective ministerial responsibility vary. In the United Kingdom, governments may be occasionally defeated in votes on relatively minor aspects of their policies. This constitutes an embarrassment to the government but does not lead to its downfall. However, a vote of 'no confidence' passed by the House of Commons would result in the government's resignation and a general election. In Germany a different procedure applies. The *Bundestag* is required to pass what is known as a 'constructive vote of no confidence' in order to oust the government. This entails a vote of no confidence in the chancellor coupled with the selection of a replacement (who is required to obtain an absolute majority vote in the *Bundestag*).

Individual ministerial responsibility is concerned with the relationship between an individual minister and the legislature. Legislatures may seek the resignation of individual ministers when errors or shortcomings are committed either by a minister or by civil servants acting in his or her name. The procedure governing individual responsibility varies. In the United Kingdom, individual ministerial responsibility is effected by the ancient penalty of reducing the salary of a minister whose actions are disapproved of. If such a vote were passed, the minister would either resign or the opposition would table a 'no confidence' motion in the government as a whole.

see also...

Accountability; Parliamentary system of government; Presidential system of government

Nationalism

Nationalism is a sentiment underpinning a people's desire to exercise control over their own political affairs. Those who live in a particular locality are united by a desire to be independent of other nations and live under a political system they control. This unity may be based on a common ethnic identity or cultural heritage (including language and literature) or be grounded on a sense of shared citizenship that may transcend ethnic or cultural differences. Nation state is the term used to describe the political community that arises when the boundaries of nation and state are the same.

Nationalism may justify attempts by conquered or colonised countries or those dominated either economically or politically by another country to shake off the burden of foreign domination and attain self-government. Post-war history contains numerous examples of national identity being the motivating force for movements seeking the establishment of self-governing states. It inspired independence movements in African countries directed against European colonial powers. In Latin America it was the main force behind anti-American movements in many countries, including Cuba and Nicaragua. The desire to establish a self-governing state has considerable influence on the contemporary politics of Canada and Spain where national minorities (the Quebeckers, Catalans and Basques) desire self-government. In the United Kingdom, the demand for Scottish and Welsh home rule resulted in devolution legislation being enacted in 1998.

Nationalism may be a progressive force when it seeks the liberation of subjugated peoples from oppressive, foreign rule. However, it may also be a reactionary movement. The love of one's country (or patriotism) may lead to the hatred of other foreign peoples or races, termed xenophobia. Nationalism was the justification for 'ethnic cleansing' (or genocide) carried out in Bosnia–Hercegovina by the Bosnian Serbs against the Bosnian Muslims in 1992 and subsequently by the Serbs against ethnic Albanians in Kosovo in 1999.

see also...

Colonialism; Devolution; European Union; Federal system of government; Globalisation; Racism; State

New public management

New public management refers to a series of reforms that have sought to remodel the way in which public policy is implemented and has led to the fragmentation of government, with public policy being implemented by a range of agencies rather than being the preserve of bodies that function as arms of the state. This approach is especially identified with the new right.

New public management embraces a number of key features. It is rooted in the new right's support for the free market, one consequence of which is to question the desirability of service provision by the public sector. It has sought to reorganise the operations of public sector agencies through the use of management techniques associated with the private sector such as performance indicators, business plans and a shift of emphasis towards the attainment of objectives at the expense of compliance with bureaucratic rules and procedures. It has emphasised the importance of value for money being provided by those who provide public services: this may be secured by a number of initiatives including procedures to enable the private sector to compete for the right to deliver services that formerly were solely associated with the public sector through the process of contracting out.

The emphasis on efficiency, value for money and quality of service are integral aspects of new public management that seeks to transform citizens into consumers whose power rests not on the political sanction of accountability but, rather, on their ability to shop around and go elsewhere if a public service is not being provided efficiently. New public management is also identified with the twin forces of centralisation and decentralisation: this entails organisational goals being set by central government (whose attainment may also be measured by centrally set performance targets) while leaving their attainment to agency heads who possess considerable operational freedom but who must operate within a budget which is also centrally determined.

see also...

Bureaucracy; Conservatism; New right

New right

The term 'new right' refers to a body of ideas that underpinned the policies pursued by a number of conservative parties in the 1980s, most notably in governments led by Margaret Thatcher (born 1925) in the United Kingdom and Ronald Reagan (born 1911) in America.

New right policies were based on two specific traditions. The first of these was termed 'neo-liberalism'. This version of economic liberalism was rooted in classical liberal ideas and sought to reduce the activities of the state whose frontiers would be 'rolled back' by the application of policies such as privatisation and reduced levels of government spending on functions such as welfare provision. This aspect of new right thinking voiced support for private enterprise and the free market and led to Keynesian economics (which regarded unemployment as the key problem to be addressed by economic policy) being replaced by new economic methods such as monetarism (which identified inflation as the main social evil which would be reduced by controlling the money supply). It was argued that government intervention in the economy led to inefficiency but that economic growth, employment, productivity and widespread prosperity would be secured if it ceased its attempts to regulate wages and prices.

The second basis of new right thinking was termed 'neo-conservatism'. This entailed a number of ideas that included social authoritarianism. This asserted that contemporary social problems such as crime, disorder, hooliganism, indiscipline among young people and moral decay were caused by the decline of 'traditional' values that had been replaced by permissive attitudes and disrespect for authority. It endorsed a 'law and order' response to social problems and demanded a return to traditional forms of authority such as the family.

Neo-liberalism and neo-conservatism are not necessarily compatible since the former emphasises self-reliance that might result in selfish behaviour whereas the latter views individuals as citizens with a range of civic obligations to fulfil.

see also...

Conservatism; Freedom; Liberalism; Privatisation

Parliamentary system of government

In a parliamentary system of government, the executive branch of government is drawn from the legislature and is also collectively accountable to this body for its actions. The office of head of state is separate from that of chief executive, the latter being the leader of the largest political party (or coalition of parties) commanding support in the legislature, who is called upon by the head of state to form a government. Its tenure in office is dependent on retaining the legislature's support and chief executives typically possess the ability to recommend the dissolution of the legislature to the head of state which triggers a general election. Countries including the United Kingdom and Germany have this form of government.

In the United Kingdom, the prime minister, members of the cabinet and junior ministers are members of parliament (most being drawn from the House of Commons). The government operates with the consent of parliament and especially the House of Commons, which possesses the ultimate sanction, that of passing a motion of 'no confidence' in it which requires it to resign. This happened in 1979 when the House of Commons expressed no confidence in the Labour government headed by James Callaghan.

In Germany, the chancellor is appointed from the largest party in the *Bundestag* (or the one that is able to construct a coalition possessing a majority in that house). The chancellor possesses considerable power, which includes control over economic policy, defence and foreign affairs and the appointment of ministers who constitute the federal government.

Executive domination of the legislature often gives prime ministers considerable power in such systems of government. There are, however, limitations to this. A government with a small, or no, majority may have to rely on members drawn from other parties to sustain it in office. In this circumstance the prime minister may have to agree to demands made by those on whom the government is forced to rely or risk defeat.

see also...

Cabinet; Coalition government; Head of state; Ministerial responsibility; Presidential system of government

Participation

Participation entails citizens being able to play a part in the political affairs of a country. Elections are a key mechanism to achieving this objective. In some liberal democracies voting is compulsory: this is the case in Australia and Belgium, for example. In others, such as the United Kingdom or America, it is optional. The extent to which citizens exercise their right to vote where this is optional is one indicator of the 'health' of that system of government. A high level of voter participation (sometimes referred to as 'turnout') might suggest enthusiasm by members of the public to involve themselves in the affairs of government in their country and in more general terms imply support for the political system that operates there.

Low turnouts may result in public policy failing to represent the national interest. If public opinion is imperfectly represented, governments may be swayed to act at the behest of organised minorities. Lack of popular involvement in the affairs of government may further pave the way for totalitarianism in which the public are frozen out of participation in government.

In most liberal democracies, participation extends beyond enabling citizens to vote or stand for election to public office and enables them to play a role in the day-to-day conduct of political affairs. Participation is frequently confused with consultation. This involves mechanisms whereby the general public is able to make its views known to those who take decisions. The key feature of consultation is that policy makers are not bound to follow the opinions expressed to them: they agree to listen but are not required to act in accordance with them. Participation, however, entails a change in the power relationship between citizens and policy makers. It is thus more radical than consultation since power is shared with the general public and policy making becomes a joint exercise involving governors and the governed. However, the lack of information in the hands of the general public might make meaningful discussion impossible.

see also...

Elections; Liberal democracy; Totalitarian

Pluralism

Pluralism suggests that power is widely distributed within society rather than being located in only one centre. This is a key characteristic of liberal democratic political systems in which power can be openly competed for rather than being concentrated in the hands of a small group of people who constitute a ruling elite.

Some pluralist theorists emphasise the importance that pressure groups have in liberal democratic political systems. These are viewed as a key mechanism through which public opinion can influence the decision-making process. Thus a pluralist society is one in which citizens are organised into a variety of interest groups that compete with each other. This process occurs within a state that is viewed as being neutral (in the sense of being independent of class interests) and is superintended by the government that adjudicates in the constant competition existing between competing groups and interests, seeking to assert the public interest. Decisions thus reflect the process of bargaining and conciliation between diverse bodies. Pluralist theorists are, however, divided as to whether the government is merely an arbiter of intergroup disputes or whether it is itself a key actor in the negotiating process, in which it acts in a manner similar to a pressure group, pursuing its own interests as well as responding to demands from outside.

A problem may arise, however, in a society in which a very wide range of groups emerge, some of which hold diametrically opposing views. The processes of consultation, bargaining and conciliation may be long and drawn out. The decision-making process may stagnate which means that governments find it difficult, or impossible, to take any decisions. This situation (which regards all interests being on an equal footing) is known as 'hyperpluralism'. However, the tendency for some groups to be more powerful than others (because of factors such as having privileged access to government) enables them to dominate the policy-making process and reduce the likelihood of stagnation occurring.

see also...

Authority; Elite; Liberal democracy; Marxism–Leninism; Power; Pressure group; State

Political culture

Political culture refers to an underlying set of values held by most people who live in a particular country concerning political behaviour, one important aspect of which is the degree of trust that citizens have in their political leaders. This implies that within a country there is a tendency for the majority of persons to think, feel and act in a similar manner concerning the conduct of political affairs. But these sentiments may be different from the core values held by citizens elsewhere.

Liberal democratic political systems embrace a wide range of similar features. However, within a common framework, political behaviour in each is subject to wide variation. For example, in France there is a wide degree of tolerance for conflict as a means of settling political disputes. In Sweden, the spirit of compromise guides the actions of key participants to the political process. In the United Kingdom, there is a tradition of evolutionary rather than revolutionary change. These variations derive from political culture.

The process that underlies the formulation of a political culture is subject to debate. Liberal theorists suggest that a country's political culture is fashioned by its unique historical development and that its underlying values are transmitted across the generations by a process termed 'political socialisation'. Agencies such as the family, schools, the media and political parties are responsible for instructing citizens in such beliefs and attitudes. Marxists, however, view political culture as an artificial creation rather than the product of history. It is seen as an ideological weapon through which society is indoctrinated to accept views that are in the interests of its dominant classes. From this perspective public support for elections as the main way to change the government or public policy is an attitude deliberately manufactured by society's ruling elite, fearful of alternative methods to achieve these ends (such as riots or revolution) that may produce radical change.

see also...

Elections; Ideology; Liberal democracy; Marxism–Leninism; Media

Political party

A political party is an organisation with a formal structure that competes for the control of government. The terms 'major' and 'minor' reflect the level of support secured by parties in a political system. Major parties generally obtain a large degree of electoral support and compete for control of the national government. Minor parties do not generally expect to win national elections but may secure power at local, regional or state level.

Political parties perform a variety of functions that benefit the operations of liberal democratic political systems. They recruit and select candidates for public office at all levels of the machinery of government and organise support for governments. The reliance of candidates on the party organisation implies a situation of dependency in which those who are elected to public office are expected to follow the party line thus providing governments with organised support. Parties enable members of the general public to participate in public affairs since those who join them are able to influence party policy. Parties may also simplify the conduct of political affairs. They do this by transforming the claims put forward by individuals and groups into programmes that can be put before the electorate. This is known as the 'aggregation of interests' and involves a process in which a wide range of demands are given a degree of coherence by being incorporated into a party platform or manifesto. One consequence of this is to transform parties into 'broad churches' that seek to maximise their level of support by incorporating the claims of a wide cross-section of society, thereby securing national harmony across social, religious or regional divisions.

However, the role of parties in liberal democratic political system varies. In America candidates for public office often promote themselves through personal organisations, even if they latterly attach themselves to a party.

see also...

Consensus politics; Dealignment; First-past-the-post system of voting; Liberal democracy; Political system; Proportional representation; Psephology

Political spectrum

The term political spectrum is used to place different political ideologies in relationship to each other thereby enabling the similarities and differences that exist between them to be identified.

The various political ideologies are grouped under the broad headings of 'left', 'right' and 'centre'. The right of fascism and conservatism, the centre consists of liberalism and social democracy and the left is comprised of socialism, communism and anarchism. Anarchism is located on the far left of the political spectrum and fascism is on the far right. This terminology was derived from the French Revolution in the late eighteenth century: the left was associated with revolution while the right was identified with reaction.

The terms 'right', 'left' and 'centre' lack precise definition but are used broadly to indicate the stances that the different ideologies adopt towards political, economic and social change. Historically, the right opposed this, preferring tradition and the established order of the past. The left endorsed change as a necessary development designed to improve the human condition. The centre was also associated with change, but wished to introduce this gradually within the existing economic and political framework that the left sought to abolish as a prerequisite to establishing an improved society.

The political spectrum is concerned with ideologies not with the political systems or practices with which they may be associated. Communism and fascism (which are on the opposite ends of the political spectrum) are both associated with totalitarian political systems in which citizens are deprived of a wide range of civil and political liberties and in which personal freedom is sacrificed to the common interests that are defined by the state. However, the nature of the society with which these two ideologies is associated is entirely different.

see also...

Anarchism; Civil rights; Communism; Conservatism; Fascism; Ideology; Liberalism; Social democracy; Socialism; Totalitarian

Political system

A political system is the constitutional framework through which demands are articulated and decisions are made. It has no physical dimension or formal existence but consists of the institutions, processes and relationships involved in the processes of agenda setting, policy formulation and decision making.

In liberal democratic political systems, demands by the public can be made through a number of channels, including political parties, pressure groups, the media, elections and extra-parliamentary political action. The suggestions put forward in this manner are key aspects of the agenda for the consideration of the formal institutions of government (the legislature, judiciary, executive and bureaucracy), which may also put forward policy proposals of their own. They determine whether to act on demands that are presented to them and if so through what means. Actions involve repealing contentious legislation, enacting new laws or taking policy or budgetary decisions.

The term 'system' implies that the component parts that shape decision making form part of an integrated structure, in which stability is secured by the actions undertaken by governments broadly matching the demands placed upon it by public opinion, however this is articulated. If this fails to be the case, disequilibrium may occur in which demands outstrip a government's willingness or ability to match them. This may result in revolution.

Political systems can be distinguished from each other in a number of ways. This process of differentiation is termed classification. There are three broad types of political systems – liberal democratic, communist and totalitarian. The extent of civil rights in liberal democratic political systems facilitates a wider degree of public participation in political affairs than is permitted in the other two systems.

see also...

Agenda setting; Civil rights; Communism; Extra-parliamentary political activity; Ideology; Liberal democracy; Marxism–Leninism; Participation; Totalitarian

Political toleration

Political toleration concerns the rules of conduct governing political activity and suggests the existence of a line determining what is acceptable political behaviour and what the state is justified in prohibiting.

Political toleration is an essential aspect of liberal democratic political systems, underpinning civil rights that include the freedom of expression and association. However, all liberal democracies impose restrictions on political activity governing, e.g., what members of political parties can say and the methods they use.

One justification for imposing restrictions on political activity is where parties fail to support the basic principles underlying liberal democracy: thus it might achieve power through the ballot box but once installed into power will transform a country's political system into a totalitarian one. The 1947 Italian Constitution banned the re-formation of the Fascist Party on these grounds while the 1958 French constitution stipulated that political parties must respect the principles of national sovereignty and democracy.

The doctrines put forward by a political party may, further, be viewed as threatening not merely to a country's political system but to the very existence of the state itself and justify limits on political activity. Fear of the Soviet Union and communism was prominent in America during the 1950s. The American Communist Party was banned by the 1954 Communist Control Act and perceived sympathy for communism led to discriminatory actions against individuals such as dismissal from employment.

The methods used by political organisations may also justify curbs on political activity. Organisations whose views, opinions or statements offend other citizens (and may possibly provoke violence against them) may be subject to restrictions. Groups which actually carry out acts of violence to further their political objectives are also likely to be the subject of constraints.

see also...

Civil rights; Communism; Liberal democracy; Terrorism; Totalitarian

Populism

Populism advocates the pursuance of policies supported by majority public opinion. These concerns and the values that underpin them are not derived from any coherent set of political beliefs but are widely varied, although a common strand is that the concerns that are articulated in populist rhetoric are depicted as resting on 'common sense' assumptions. Typically populist politics directs its appeal to the masses over the heads of other established social and political institutions (such as the family, social class, political parties and trade unions) by focusing on a cause that can be depicted as harmful and contrary to the best interests of mass public opinion. This appeal is especially directed at those at the lower end of the social scale although the leaders of such movements tend to be drawn from higher up the social ladder.

Examples of populist movements include the America People's Party of the 1890s, which voiced the concerns of farmers in the western and southern states and demanded the increased coinage of silver. Populism is particularly identified with Juan Péron (1895–1974), the President of Argentina 1946–55 and 1973–74. His power rested on his ability to mobilise the poorer elements in society against the institutions of the state. As with fascism, populism is often identified with the strong leadership of a charismatic figure and a distrust of representative institutions.

In western liberal democracies, populist politics are often identified with extreme right wing political parties who suggest that the problems of 'ordinary' members of the general public are due to the policies pursued by 'unrepresentative politicians' who have ignored the interests of the masses by pursuing policies such as immigration and by adopting over-liberal attitudes in areas such as law and order and social policy. Support for such views is often cultivated by selecting a target (usually a weak and vulnerable group in society) that can be scapegoated and depicted as both the root cause and embodiment of the crisis allegedly facing society.

see also...

Fascism; Media

Power

Power consists of a relationship between two parties in which one has the ability to compel the other to undertake a course of action that would not voluntarily have been carried out. The preferences of one party become binding on the other because the former has the ability to compel compliance by the threat or the use of sanctions. The desire to avoid the sanction thus ensures the obedience of one party to another. Governments may exercise power over their citizens but other political organisations (such as pressure groups and social movements) may wield power by their ability to use force or violence to further their aims.

The nature of power is a fundamental issue related to the study of politics. In *Power: A Radical View,* written in 1974, Stephen Lukes identified three dimensions to power – the one- dimensional view (which focused on whose views prevailed in decision making), the two-dimensional view (which involved examining both decision making but also non-decision making) and the three-dimensional view (which focused on the ability to control the political agenda by the ability to manipulate people's needs and preferences).

Power is different from influence, which entails the ability of those who are not participants to a policy-making process to be able to affect the content and nature of its decisions. Their ability to do so may include the intellectual weight of arguments they are able to put forward.

In liberal democracies governments possess both power and authority. They are obeyed partly because there is general consent that they have the right to govern, but also because the police, courts and penal system may be used as a sanction to force compliance to their laws. Power that is divorced from authority is likely to produce a repressive regime whose stability may be undermined by violence, disorder or revolution.

There is considerable debate concerning whether power is widely dispersed (as pluralists argue) or held by a small group of powerful individuals (as elite theorists and Marxists allege).

see also...

Authority; Elite; Liberal democracy; Marxism–Leninism; Pluralism

Presidential system of government

A presidential system of government is a political structure in which different personnel compose the executive and legislative branches. The executive branch is elected for a fixed term and also occupies the position of head of state. The legislature has no formal relationship with the executive branch of government other than its ability to remove the president through the process of impeachment and the president does not have the power to dissolve the legislature and call a general election. This system of government is found in both North and South America.

Presidential powers are limited by the need to secure the legislature's support for certain executive actions. Thus one problem faced by chief executives is how to mobilise the legislature to secure the attainment of their policy goals. This poses a particular problem in America where party loyalty in congress is relatively weak. Parochialism exerts considerable influence over the conduct of its members who are more likely to follow the president's lead when they feel this will bring them personal political benefits with their constituents but will distance themselves from the administration if they feel association with it is an electoral liability.

The position of a president is potentially weaker when the opposition party controls either or both houses of the legislature. This may give rise to a situation in which neither side will give way to the other, which is termed 'gridlock'.

Presidents possess a number of formal and informal powers to overcome problems in their relationship with legislatures. They may use the authority of their office to attain their objectives, perhaps by addressing their case directly to the public, or attempt to construct coalitions within the legislature to secure the passage of key measures. American presidents may issue executive orders which enable them to act without consulting congress.

see also...

Executive branch of government; Head of state; Legislative branch of government; Parliamentary system of government; Separation of powers

Pressure group

A pressure (or interest) group is an organisation with a formal structure, composed of a number of individuals seeking to further a common cause or interest. The main aim of pressure groups is to influence the conduct of specific areas of civic affairs (unlike political parties that seek to control all aspects of a country's policy-making process). This may be achieved through a range of activities, including constructing relationships with the executive branch of government (especially the permanent civil service), lobbying legislators, initiating legal actions in the courts or forging close links with political parties. Additionally, some groups seek to influence public opinion through the use of extra-parliamentary methods of protest and direct action. Developments such as the growth of supranational governmental organisations (such as the European Union) have further encouraged pressure groups to operate on a world stage, coordinating their activities with like-minded organisations in other countries.

There are two broad types of pressure groups. There are sectional groups (which seek to advance a cause in which members have a material interest) and promotional (or cause) groups (where the work of the group is primarily viewed as a moral concern, aiming to alter social values and attitudes). Trade unions or professional associations constitute examples of the former, while promotional groups include those seeking to secure support for concerns such as homelessness or animal welfare.

Pressure groups promote educating the public, and by enabling citizens to become involved in the process of policy making. However, they also pose problems often related to the ability of some groups commanding considerable economic resources and possessing powerful sanctions to dominate the policy-making process and ensure that their sectional concerns are elevated above the national interest.

see also...

Direct action; Executive; Extra-parliamentary political action; European Union; Judiciary; Legislature; Liberal democracy; Lobbying; Political party; Pluralism; Social movement; Third world

Privacy

Privacy may be broadly defined as the 'right to be left alone'. A fundamental issue concerns where the public's 'right to know' stops and a public person's 'right to privacy' begins. This is a particularly sensitive issue when information is obtained in dubious ways including the use of telephoto lenses or bugging devices. The boundaries between the public right to know and the privacy of an individual is often determined by the media themselves who may operate some form of code of practice. In the United Kingdom, for example, there exists a voluntary code of practice, policed by the Press Complaints Commission to whom those aggrieved by media intrusion into their private lives may appeal.

The main alternative to media self-regulation is through privacy legislation which would enable the courts to award damages when such rights are violated. Privacy legislation exists in a number of European countries: a right to privacy is recognised in both French and German law while in Denmark unauthorised photography on private property is forbidden. This issue is regulated by state governments in America.

There are, however, problems associated with privacy legislation. It is complicated to draft and may be used to prevent legitimate scrutiny by the media of the activities of public officials. It gives the judiciary a major role in determining the boundaries between privacy and freedom of speech. Its effectiveness is also limited in those countries that have it. In France, for example, the civil damages awarded are usually low and the sanction of the total stoppage of a publication is rarely used. In Germany, privacy is balanced by Article 5 of the 1949 Constitution which specifically protects the freedom of speech and of the press.

Other legislation may protect privacy. Data protection legislation typically gives the public the right to inspect personal information held on them in computer files and other databases and may insist that such personal data may prevent it being used without their consent.

see also...

Civil rights; Freedom of information; Human rights; Media

Privatisation

Privatisation was a policy favoured by the new right, consistent with its belief in the free market. After 1989 it was pursued in a number of former communist states that felt state control of industry had failed significantly to benefit the working class.

In the United Kingdom, privatisation was especially associated with denationalising many of the state-controlled industries and returning them to the private sector, thereby reducing the size of the public sector. Some industries (such as Ferranti in 1980) were sold by private sale but in others, which included British Telecom (1984), British Gas (1986) and British Airways (1987), the state's section was sold off in the form of shares offered to the public. This gave the Treasury an immediate influx of huge amounts of money and was theoretically designed to advance the concept of 'popular capitalism' in which ordinary members of the general public were able to buy shares (and receive regular dividend on them).

Privatisation also embraced contracting out and deregulation. This entailed public sector services being delivered by private sector organisations either by the service being totally divorced from government or being contracted out. In this case central or local government draws up contracts that are subject to competitive tendering and then monitors the performance of those to whom such contracts are awarded. These reforms view competition as the main way to make services become responsive to public demand that was also reflected in attempts to establish internal markets (consisting of purchasers and providers) in state-administered services such as the United Kingdom's National Health Service.

Contracting out was pursued in America after 1980. In the United Kingdom, it was imposed on local government in the 1980s and during the 1990s 'market testing' was introduced to establish the advantages of government departments contracting out a range of services to the private sector.

see also...

Conservatism; New Right; Socialism

Progressivism

Progressivism is generally identified with the centre left of the political spectrum and seeks social and political reform deemed to be beneficial to the majority of the population. These reforms are put forward within the existing framework of capitalist society and thus excludes those groups which seek revolutionary change or upheaval. Constitutional reform is a particular concern of progressive movements, whose objective is to bring government closer to the people.

In America, the progressive movement initiated a number of political reforms between 1890–1920, many of which affected state government. These included the use of referendum, which typically took the form of the petition referendum enabling a predetermined number of signatories to suspend the operation of a law passed by the state legislature that would be placed before the public at a future state election. A further reform was the initiative petition, which enabled a set number of a state's voters to put a proposed law on a ballot paper and which became law if approved by a majority of voters regardless of whether the state legislature chose to enact it. Most states have adopted some form of referendum and around half utilise the initiative petition.

Other reforms associated with American progressivism included enabling a set number of electors to recall an elected representative at either state or federal level (which has the effect of 'de-electing' this person); and the introduction of direct election of senators, civil service examinations, a method of enabling popular choice to determine the selection of candidates put forward by political parties (termed 'primary elections), and the long ballot. In congress progressive pressure succeeded in drastically reducing the power of the speaker of the house of representatives to control its actions. Progressive parties have also stood in presidential elections in 1912, 1924 and 1948, the most successful of which was the 'Bull Moose Party' led by former President Theodore Roosevelt (1858–1919).

see also...

Capitalism; Conservatism; Constitution; Political spectrum

Proportional representation

Proportional representation seeks to ensure that the wishes of the electorate are arithmetically reflected in the composition of the legislature. It is an objective rather than a specific method of election, the main forms of which are the single transferable vote and the party list system.

The single transferable vote requires a country to be divided into a number of multi-member constituencies that return more than one member to the legislature. Electors are required to number candidates in order of preference. To be elected a candidate has to secure a predetermined quota of votes. The redistribution (or transfer) of votes from one candidate to another is the key distinguishing feature of this form of proportional representation.

The other main form of proportional representation is the party list system, which seeks to ensure that parties are represented in legislative bodies in proportion to the votes cast for them. Political parties draw up lists of candidates (which may be compiled on a national or a regional basis) who are placed in order of preference. When the votes are counted, a party's representation in a legislative body arithmetically reflects the proportion of votes it obtained. In a simplistic form, a party that obtained 20% of the total national poll would be entitled to 20% of the seats in the legislature.

Hybrid electoral systems exist that seek to blend the first-past-the-post system with proportional representation. In Germany, both systems are used concurrently so minority parties that fare badly under the former system can be compensated under the latter.

Proportional representation ensures that minority parties are fairly treated and are thus provided with an inducement to operate within the conventional political system. It may secure the representation of political extremes which, once established within a legislative body, gain respectability and increase their support.

see also...

Coalition government; Consensus politics; First-past-the-post system of voting; Legislative branch of government

Psephology

Psephology is the study of voting behaviour, seeking to establish why electors vote in the way they do.

Models of voting behaviour which were developed after 1945 drew heavily on American political science. The aim of a model is to provide an explanation for voting behaviour that holds good for a significant proportion of the electorate and, additionally, applies from one generation to the next when a large number of citizens become eligible to vote for the first time, replacing former voters who have died. The Michigan model was influential and suggested that the basis of voting behaviour was an attachment formed between voters and political parties. It was perceived that an individual's association with a political party was determined by the influences encountered in his or her social relationships. Of these, the major factor was the family.

There are a number of possible factors that may constitute the underpinning of political parties, providing them with their core support. These include religion (which plays a crucial role in determining political allegiance in Northern Ireland and in parts of Germany) and local and regional influences. Examples of the latter include the Italian *Lega Nord*, the Scottish National party, *Plaid Cymru* in Wales, the *Parti Québecois* in Quebec, Canada, and the Catalan Republican Left and Basque National parties in Spain. Gender and race may also influence party affiliation. The Afro-Caribbean vote is an important constituent of the support enjoyed by the United Kingdom Labour Party and the American Democratic Party.

Social class (which consists of a group of people who possess common economic interests derived from their similar social and economic position) may also influence a voter's choice of political party. This dominated explanations of voting behaviour in the United Kingdom from 1945 until 1970 when partisan and class dealignment gave rise to new models of voting behaviour. These included issue voting, which suggested that specific topical events or policies influence political behaviour.

see also...

Dealignment; Realignment

Public opinion polls

Public opinion polls measure public opinion on specific political issues (such as the standing of the parties or to gauge public support for particular items of public policy).

Opinion polls seek to determine the views of the public by putting questions to a small group of people. There are several ways in which such a group might be selected but two main ones are the use of a random sample or a quota. The first addresses questions to a segment of the public who are chosen by a method that lacks scientific construction. In the United Kingdom, for example, a random sample might consist of every thousandth name on the register of electors in a particular parliamentary constituency. A quota sample, however, seeks to address questions to a group of people whose composition is determined in advance. By this method, questions are directed at a group who are perceived to be a cross-section of the public.

Polls are especially prominent in election campaigns. They are used to assess the views of voters on particular issues and to ask voters who they intend to support at an election. The belief that this activity may actually influence voting behaviour (for example, by creating a bandwagon effect for the party judged by the polls to be in the lead) has prompted countries such as France to ban the publication of poll results close to the actual contest.

Although opinion polls are widely used they are not consistently accurate. Some people may refuse to answer the pollsters' questions which may distort the result if such refusals are disproportionately made by one segment of electoral opinion. Polls rely on those who are questioned telling the truth or subsequently adhering to the opinions they express to the pollsters. The 'last-minute swing' phenomenon suggests that members of the general public may alter their minds and depart from a previously expressed opinion. Polls may also find accuracy difficult when the public is very evenly divided on the matter under investigation.

see also...

Elections; Liberal democracy; Referendum

Quango

A quango (quasi-autonomous non-governmental organisation) is a body that implements public policy, but is not a government department. Quangos are created by central government which fully or partially funds them. The staff employed by quangos may be civil servants but often are not. In Ireland these organisations are termed state sponsored bodies.

Quangos perform a wide range of functions. Some are executive bodies that implement public policy. Their main advantage is that the organisation is purpose built to perform a specific function. Others are advisory bodies whose main advantage is that they provide expert advice at relatively low cost. Others perform regulatory functions. In the United Kingdom, these include tribunals whose function is to adjudicate disputes between individuals without these matters being referred to the courts, whose procedures and costs may not be appropriate to the matter in hand.

These bodies possess a large degree of operational independence and may be used to avoid detailed accountability which may be equated with the constant 'interference' of politicians. Organisations that pursue commercial or quasi-commercial activities require a certain amount of freedom so that enterprise can flourish. Others that pursue non-economic tasks may also justify a relative degree of insulation from political control on the argument that the task with which they are concerned should not be subject to the constant to and fro of political debate: thus such bodies effectively depoliticise the function with which they are concerned. However, this operational freedom may result in these bodies being inadequately accountable for their actions to either the executive or legislative branches of government.

Quangos have been criticised for providing a source of patronage that enables a government to reward its supporters with paid employment rather than seeking to fill vacancies with people who are best able to perform the job.

see also...

Accountability; Bureaucracy

Racism

Racism asserts the inferiority of black people in comparison to white people. It is a social construction: such views have no factual objective or undisputable basis but instead are formed on unscientific opinion and value judgements.

The aim of racism is to justify the control that one set of individuals wishes to exert over another. It establishes (and subsequently perpetuates) an unequal relationship between white and black people in which the former exercise power and the latter are subservient. To achieve this aim, it becomes necessary to assert that the intended victims of racism are subhuman. The denial by one group of another's humanity provides a climate in which violence ranging from racial harassment to genocide (that is, the extermination of a racial group) will occur and in which prejudice and discrimination will be encountered.

There is no agreement concerning the root causes of racism. Psychological explanations of racism focus on the personality of the individual. A further explanation views history as its crucial underpinning, whereby white nations conquered black African countries during the nineteenth century. The right to exert this control was justified by social Darwinism (which asserted that the white race had evolved to a greater degree than the black race).

Marxists assert that capitalism is the source of racism. This economic system requires both the guaranteed existence of an abundant supply of labour and also mechanisms to prevent the development of class conflict. Thus Marxist analysis would assert that immigration was initially designed to secure the abundance of unskilled and semi-skilled labour and that racial prejudice was nurtured to hinder the development of class consciousness. Subsequent problems such as low wages or scarcity of employment thus resulted in members of the working class fighting themselves on racial lines rather than pooling their resources against those who benefited from an economic system that caused social injustice.

see also...

Affirmative action; Capitalism; Colonialism; Marxism–Leninism

Realignment

Realignment entails a redefinition of the relationship between political parties and key social groups within society that has a fundamental impact on their relative strength. Partisan and class dealignment, which entail the loosening of traditional bonds attaching individuals and groups to particular parties, may be the prelude of realignment.

The formation of new relationships is usually confirmed in what is termed a 'realigning election', which is seen as the start of new patterns of political behaviour. In the United Kingdom, the 1918 general election evidenced the desertion of the working class vote from the Liberal Party to Labour. The 1932 American presidential election, which witnessed the birth of the 'New Deal Coalition', was a further example of realignment. This coalition was composed of union members, ethnic minorities, liberals and intellectuals and these newly established patterns of voter loyalties provided the Democratic Party with domination over congress and the presidency for a number of subsequent decades. In both of these examples, however, the changes in voter loyalty, evidenced at the realignment elections, had been initiated earlier.

Subsequent examples of realignment have occurred. In America, the victories of Ronald Reagan (born 1911) in 1980 and 1984 were based on the existence of a new coalition. The preference of white male voters in the southern states of America for the Republican Party indicated a major shift in this group's political affiliation which developed from changes that had taken place in the 1970s. In the United Kingdom, the era of Conservative Party dominance (1979–1997) rested in part on the defection of relatively affluent members of the working class in south eastern England (who were characterised by working in the private sector and owning their own homes) to vote Conservative. However, neither of these changes has been sufficient to bring about total political domination for the parties that benefited from them. In the United Kingdom the Conservatives were voted out of office in the 1997 general election.

see also...

Dealignment; Psephology

Referendum

Referendums give the general public the opportunity to vote on specific policy issues in order to indicate their approval or disapproval of a course of action. They are an important aspect of direct democracy and are used in varying degrees by liberal democracies, Switzerland making considerable use of them.

Referendums provide a mechanism to permit mass public involvement in major policy issues (perhaps of considerable constitutional or importance). In Ireland proposals to amend the constitution, following enactment by the *Oireachtas* (parliament), must be submitted to a referendum. Recent examples in the United Kingdom include the devolution proposals for Scotland and Wales in 1997 and the vote to evidence popular approval in Northern Ireland for the 'Good Friday' peace accord in 1998. In some countries the public has the right both to call a referendum and to exercise some control over its content. In New Zealand, for example, the 1993 Citizens Initiated Referenda Act gave 10% of registered electors the opportunity to initiate a non-binding referendum on any subject.

However, referendums may devalue the role performed by legislative bodies by reducing their ability to determine the content of public policy. The power of the executive branch of government may also be limited by the use of referendum since governments may be forced to follow public opinion at the expense of their ability to lead it. The general public may be unable to understand the complexities of the issue that is the subject of a referendum.

A referendum is not always associated with the progressive political intention of bringing government closer to the people. Dictators may use them instead of representative institutions such as parliament, asserting such bodies are unnecessary since the people are directly consulted on government policy. The use of referendum by Germany's Nazi government (1933–45) resulted in the 1949 German Constitution prohibiting their further use.

see also...

Executive branch of government; Legislative branch of government; Liberal democracy

Representation

Representation enables public opinion to be involved in decision making. This may be achieved in a number of ways, including consultative mechanisms or cooption. In liberal democratic political systems representation specifically refers to the process of electing members to legislative bodies who theoretically represent the interests of those who voted them into office, thereby providing a link between government and governed.

The nature of this relationship varies. It usually takes the form of territorial representation whereby a legislator represents a specific geographic area and its inhabitants. However, an alternative form of representation, functional representation, exists in some countries in which legislators represent sectional interests. The Irish *Seanad* is constituted on this basis whereby some members are chosen to reflect vocational interests.

The extent to which those elected to public office faithfully represent public opinion is a key concern of representation. Those elected to public office may fulfil the role either of delegate or of representative. A delegate is an elected official who follows the instructions of the electorate as and when these are given. This contrasts to a representative whose actions are determined by that person's conscience and not by instructions delivered by voters. Representatives are subject to no formal restraints on their actions once elected, which may result in their failing to act in accordance with public opinion. Parties may distort the relationship between an elected official and his or her electors. While in office, party discipline may force an official to sacrifice locality to party if these interests do not coincide.

A further view of representation (termed characteristic representation) suggests that the institution of a representative government can only truly reflect public opinion when they contain members drawn from all key social groups within society in proportion to their strength.

see also...

Corporatism; Legislative branch of government; Liberal democracy; Political party

Rule of law

The rule of law is a fundamental constitutional principle in liberal democracies that asserts the supremacy of the law as an instrument which governs both the actions of individual citizens in their relationships with each other and also controls the conduct of the state towards them.

The rule of law suggests that citizens can only be punished by the state using formalised procedures when they have transgressed the law and that all citizens will be treated in the same way when they commit wrongdoings. Nobody is 'above the law' and the punishments meted out for similar crimes should be the same, regardless of who has committed them. This suggests that the law is applied dispassionately and is not subject to the biases and prejudices of those who enforce it. Additionally, all citizens should be aware of the contents of the law. The rule of law, therefore, provides a powerful safeguard to the citizen against arbitrary actions committed by the state and its officials and is best guaranteed by a judiciary which is independent of the other branches of government.

This principle may be grounded in common law (which is the situation in the United Kingdom) or be incorporated into a codified constitution. In America, the freedom of citizens from arbitrary actions undertaken by government is enshrined in the Constitution (most notably the 5th and 14th amendments) which lays down the procedure which must be followed when citizens are accused of criminal actions.

However, most liberal democratic states deviate from the strict application of the rule of law. Factors including financial means, class, race or gender may play an influential part in determining whether a citizen who transgresses the law is proceeded against by the state and may also have a major bearing on the outcome of any trial. Additionally, governments may depart from the rule of law when emergencies occur.

see also...

Capitalism; Constitution; Federal system of government; Judicial branch of government; Liberal democracy; Marxism–Leninism; Separation of powers

Separation of powers

The separation of powers suggests that each branch of government (namely the legislature, executive and judiciary) should perform a defined range of functions, possess autonomy in relationship to the other two and be staffed by personnel different from those of the others. This principle was advocated by Baron Montesquieu (1689–1755) in his work *De l'Esprit des Lois*, written in 1748. His key concern was to suggest ways to avoid tyranny and he asserted that this was most effectively avoided if the three branches of government were separate rather than power being concentrated in the executive branch of government.

The American Constitution was considerably influenced by this principle and set out the functions and composition of the three branches of government. An important example of the independence of the branches provided for in the Constitution is that, the American president is not permitted to be a member of congress.

However, one difficulty with the separation of powers is that if it were strictly followed each branch of government would be accountable only to itself. This might result in insufficient restraints being imposed over their actions, enabling each the potential to act in an arbitrary (that is, unreasonable or dictatorial) fashion. The American Constitution thus sought to avoid this situation from occurring by providing for the fragmentation of political power through a system of checks and balances whereby the key functions and operations performed by one branch were subject to scrutiny by the others. Thus the president's power to appoint members of the executive branch of government is restricted by the requirement that senior appointees are subject to the approval ('confirmation') of the senate. This principle extended to the relationships within the branches of government so that, in the case of congress, the actions of one of its two houses could be restrained by the other.

see also...

Accountability; Constitution; Executive branch of government; Judicial branch of government; Judicial review; Legislative branch of government; Power

Sleaze

Sleaze describes the abuse of power by elected public officials who improperly exploit their office for personal gain, party advantage (which may especially benefit party leaders) or for sexual motives. The term also embraces attempts to cover up such inappropriate behaviour either by those guilty of misconduct or by their political colleagues. Accusations of 'sleaze' have exerted a major influence on politics in a number of liberal democratic political systems since the 1990s.

In the United Kingdom, the government's emphasis on the need for a return to conservative traditional values of self-discipline and the importance of the family in its 'back to basics' policy of 1993 was undone by revelations that a number of members of the government were engaging in extra-marital affairs. A further problem was the 'cash for questions' accusation in 1994 that a small number of Conservative members of parliament had accepted money to table parliamentary questions. This resulted in the appointment of a Committee on Standards in Public Life, whose recommendations included establishing an independent parliamentary commissioner.

In America, sleaze took the form of allegations that President Clinton had a sexual relationship with Monica Lewinsky. Initially, both Clinton and Lewinsky swore on oath that they had not had an affair. However, doubt was subsequently cast on the truthfulness of these denials and Clinton admitted to having had an 'inappropiate' physical relationship with her. The report of a special counsel, Kenneth Starr, to the House of Representative's Judiciary Committee, accused the president of perjury, abuse of power, obstruction of justice and witness tampering. In December 1998 the House of Representatives' Judicial Committee approved four articles of impeachment, two of which were subsequently endorsed by the House of Representatives. This decision resulted in a trial before the senate at which Clinton was acquitted in February 1999.

see also...

Lobbying; Presidential system of government

Social democracy

Social democracy rests within the reformist (or revisionist) tradition of socialism. It suggests that social inequalities can be addressed by an enhanced level of state intervention within the existing structure of the capitalist economic system. The influence of social democracy was increased after 1945 when capitalism was seen to be bringing many benefits to working-class people (such as a rising standard of living and social mobility) in a number of countries that in turn tended to reduce the hostility between the social classes.

Lord John Maynard Keynes (1883–1946) was especially influential in the development of social democratic politics. He argued that a market economy subject to an enhanced degree of state intervention to manage demand could provide an effective solution to the problem of unemployment. His policy of demand management was adopted by a number of socialist parties as an alternative to state control of the economy.

Social democracy also sought to remove social problems affecting the poorer members of society through the establishment of a welfare state. This was a mechanism to provide for the redistribution of wealth within society, since the welfare state would be financed by public money obtained through the taxation of income so that the rich would contribute towards addressing the health and welfare needs of the poor. Social democracy was also associated with other policies designed to improve the access of poorer members of society to a range of services such as housing and education.

There are a number of key differences between fundamentalists and social democrats. The latter view nationalisation as one means among many that may be used to secure state influence over the workings of the economy. Fundamentalists assert that social democratic policies such as the welfare state serve not to create a socialist society but, rather, to hinder the development of class consciousness thereby perpetuating capitalism.

see also...

Capitalism; Communism; Equality; Marxism–Leninism; Socialism

Social movement

Social movement seeks to promote political change from outside of the conventional political system. Such movements are associated with the left wing of the political spectrum but have substituted the traditional Marxist goal of achieving the overthrow of capitalism attainable through a working-class revolution with a range of tactics that seek to transform society by redefining social values and thus culturally undermining this economic system. Social movements typically operate outside mainstream political institutions and their tactics are dominated by non-conventional forms of political activity, including direct action.

Social movements have some similarities with pressure groups but can be differentiated from them in a number of important ways. They are loosely organised, generally lacking a formal structure and the focus of their concern is broader: rather than concentrate on one specific policy area, their concern is to instil new moral values within society. These operate on an international stage rather than being confined to any one particular country and the coordination of their activities has been aided by modern means of communication such as the internet.

Social movements may embrace the activities of pressure groups whose specific aims are compatible with this overall objective. For example, the British Campaign for Nuclear Disarmament would be located under the umbrella of the Peace Movement.

The environmental movement is an important example of a contemporary social movement. It has succeeded in bringing together a range of groups engaged in counter-cultural protest (such as new age travellers) and those opposed to hunting, live animal exports, motorway construction and pollution. These seemingly disparate, single-issue bodies are united by a social vision that rejects the culture of advanced capitalist society. All stand opposed to what they view as an alliance of developers, business, the construction industry and government.

see also...

Direct action; Marxism–Leninism; Political spectrum Pressure group

Socialism

Socialism arose in reaction to the exploitive nature of capitalism. It rejects a society in which inequalities in the distribution of wealth and political power result in social injustice and is committed to the ideal of equality. Socialists seek a society in which cooperation and fraternity replace the divisions based on class lines that characterise capitalist societies. There is, however, considerable disagreement concerning both the nature of an egalitarian society and how it would be created. These stem from the diverse traditions embraced by socialism.

The roots of socialism include: the economic theories of David Ricardo (who suggested that the interests of capital and labour were opposed); the reforming activites of Robert Owen (who advocated the ownership of the means of production by small groups of producers organised into societies based upon the spirit of cooperation); the Christian impulse (which was relevant to socialism through its concern for the poor and the early experiences of Christians living in a society in which property was held in common); and the writings of Karl Marx (1818–1883) and Friedrich Engels (1820–1895), who asserted that inequality was rooted in private property ownership and the class system that derived from this.

The varied impulses that influenced socialism explain the differences within it. A key division is between fundamentalist and reformist socialism (or social democracy). Fundamentalist socialists believe that state control of all means of production is indispensable to the creation of an egalitarian society and is thus viewed as their main political objective. They reject the free market and, instead, have historically endorsed the centralised planning of the economy and the nationalisation (or 'socialisation') of key industries to achieve this goal.

Reformist (or revisionist) socialists, however, believe that an egalitarian society can be created by reforming the capitalist system rather than abolishing it.

see also...

Capitalism; Communism; Equality; Marxism–Leninism; Social democracy

Soundbite

Soundbites consist of a short self-contained phrase or sentence through which a politician seeks to communicate views, opinions, attitudes or personality traits to the general public. The term was first used in America in the 1960s but has subsequently been applied on both sides of the Atlantic.

Soundbites may be used to provide the public with a brief statement that encapsulates a politician's or political party's stance on a particular policy issue, seeking to provide the public with an image associating a politician or political party with a particular course of action. In this case they are similar to an advertising jingle. An example of a soundbite with this intention was the statement in 1993 by the then United Kingdom Home Secretary, Michael Howard, that 'prison works', which was intended to convey the impression of a government that intended that a tough line on crime should be taken involving the use of imprisonment rather than non-custodial forms of punishment.

Soundbites may also be used by politicians to summarise those personality traits that they believe might enhance their popular appeal. An example of this was the statement made by the former Prime Minister of the United Kingdom, Margaret Thatcher, in 1980 that 'the lady's not for turning' in response to suggestions that her economic policies should be adjusted to combat increasing unemployment and deepening economic recession.

The use of soundbites has been prompted by the role played by the media (especially television) in political affairs. The time given to political affairs is limited and it is thus essential that politicians use the time at their disposal to maximum effect. Their use has additionally been encouraged by a perception that the attention span of the general public is extremely limited and that anything beyond a brief statement will not be absorbed.

A major problem with soundbites is that politics becomes more concerned with presentation than content.

see also...

Media; Spin doctor

Sovereignty

Sovereignty entails a body possessing unrestricted power. In contemporary politics it has two dimensions: internal sovereignty refers to the existence of a supreme legal or political authority that has the power to make decisions binding on all its citizens; external sovereignty refers to self-determination and suggests that a state has the ability to control its own affairs without interference from outside bodies and countries.

Internal sovereignty is divided within federal states. In countries including America, Australia, Canada and Germany, the national government may enact legislation in certain areas of activity while other matters are regulated by the states or provinces into which these countries are divided. In unitary countries such as the United Kingdom and France, sovereignty is not divided but resides in the institutions of national government that have the sole right to regulate these nations' affairs.

External sovereignty has been eroded by the increasing interdependence of nations. The emergence of supranational organisations such as the European Union and international bodies such as the United Nations, restrict the freedom of action of their members (and sometimes non-members). Agreements on trade limit the ability of participating countries to pursue tariff protection. Broader agreements have also been made to regulate the world's trading system through international actions which include the Group of Seven (G-7) summit meetings. These initiatives impinge on the control that individual nations exert over their economic policies.

The growth of multinational companies also limits the sovereignty of individual states, since these companies possess considerable influence over the operations of the government in the countries in which they are located.

see also...

Dependency; European Union; Federal system of government; Globalisation; Nationalism; Sovereignty of parliament; Third world; Unitary system of government

Sovereignty of parliament

The sovereignty of parliament implies that parliament may pass any legislation it wishes and the implementation of this legislation cannot then be challenged by any other body within the state (such as a court or a local authority). This concept is at the heart of the United Kingdom's system of government. Initially, this doctrine was designed to provide for the pre-eminence of parliament over the monarchy.

The importance attached to the sovereignty of parliament was illustrated by the manner in which the 1998 Human Rights Act operates. This legislation incorporated the European Convention of Human Rights into United Kingdom law, providing a bill of rights whose guarantees were designed to be embodied into all subsequent law passed by parliament. In some countries (such as Canada), human rights legislation empowers judges to strike down any legislation that conflicts with these basic principles. However, in order to square this legislation with the sovereignty of parliament, this situation does not apply in the United Kingdom. Under the 1998 legislation, judges were empowered to declare a law passed by parliament to be 'incompatible with the convention'. Although it was assumed that declarations of this nature by the courts would induce the government and parliament to introduce corrective measures speedily to bring such complained of legislation into line with the Convention of Human Rights, there was nothing to prevent either of these bodies from ignoring such rulings.

A further aspect of the sovereignty of parliament is that one parliament cannot bind a successor to a course of action. Any law passed by one parliament can be amended or repealed subsequently by a successor. Thus while Britain's membership of the European Union asserts that European law has precedence over that enacted by the United Kingdom parliament, this apparent undermining of the sovereignty of parliament is addressed by the theoretical ability of a future parliament to withdraw Britain from this supranational arrangement.

see also...

European Union; Human rights; Sovereignty

Spin doctor

A spin doctor is concerned with ensuring that the policies of a political party are effectively presented to the electorate in order to ensure their maximum popular appeal. The term was first used in America in the 1980s and the United Kingdom Labour Party's success at the 1997 general election was heavily influenced by the manner in which spin doctors were able to manage or manipulate the reporting activities of the media, particularly the newspapers, so that their policy and criticisms of the Conservative government received favourable coverage. Following Labour's victory at the 1997 general election, a number of these spin doctors were employed in order to secure governmental control of the media agenda so that journalists would be placed in the position of responding to government initiatives rather than putting forward proposals of their own. The main advantage of this for the government was that it gave it the appearance of being in control of situations.

The position occupied by spin doctors as middlemen between politicians and the electorate provides them with considerable power, since to perform their functions effectively requires them to exercise much control over political affairs and in particular a party's media relations. This may have disadvantageous consequences for the operations of liberal democracies. Spin doctors might feel it necessary to dominate elected politicians to the extent of devising policy proposals that they deem to have popular appeal or imposing censorship on the media. If a spin doctor acts for a party in government this may take the form of seeking to control media activities by bullying journalists into reporting the activities of the government favourably, or denying access to government sources to journalists or publications that adopt a critical stance to it. Further, the emphasis they place on presentation and image may become a substitute for policy so the attention of electors becomes diverted from the contents of government proposals to be focused instead on issues such as delivery, appearance or image.

see also...

Agenda setting; Legislative branch of government; Liberal democracy; Media

State

A state consists of a wide range of permanent official institutions (such as the bureaucracy, police, courts, military, parliament and local government) that are responsible for the organisation of communal life within specific geographic boundaries, usually referred to as a 'country' or 'nation' and within which the state enjoys sovereignty. Decisions taken in the name of the state are binding on all members of that society and may, if necessary, be enforced by the legitimate use of power to prevent, restrain or punish breaches of the law.

There is a vast spectrum of views concerning the operations of the state. Liberal analysis suggests that the state is neutral and independent of any class interests. It arises out of the voluntary agreement of its members and serves impartially to mediate the conflicts that arise within society, seeking to promote the national interest above sectional concerns. Elite theorists, however, suggest political power is wielded by the ruling elite whose interests are maintained and advanced by the state. Marxism identifies this ruling elite as the economically powerful, the bourgeoisie, and views the state as a mechanism that will mediate in the conflict between capital and labour (which they assert to be inevitable) in order to sustain class exploitation and profit accumulation. Managerialist perspectives suggest that the state enjoys autonomy from social classes in advanced capitalist societies and point to the power wielded by bureaucracies in controlling its operations. Structuralist accounts view the state as representing the balance of class forces in a society at a specific point in time. The new right focuses on the activities undertaken by the state and argues that its interference in the everyday lives of people ought to be reduced.

The term 'state' is different from the term 'government'. The latter refers to the institutions that are concerned with making, implementing and enforcing laws.

see also...

Elite; Judicial branch of government; Liberalism; Local government; Marxism–Leninism; Nationalism; New right; Sovereignty

Terrorism

Terrorism involves the use of violence in order to achieve political objectives. The 1974 United Kingdom Prevention of Terrorism Act defined the term as 'the use of violence for political ends and includes any use of violence for the purpose of putting the public or any section of it in fear'.

Violence can be used to achieve many different objectives. These include the revolutionary aim of overthrowing a state or to achieve reforms that can be secured within a country's existing economic, political or social system but which the government is unwilling to enact. Here violence is used in an attempt to force the government to introduce them. Violence may also be guided by liberational objectives, seeking to rid a country of foreign rule. The use of violence to achieve this objective has met with a number of successes across the world, most notably in opposition to colonial rule exercised by European countries in Africa and Asia. Violence may also be sponsored by states. This may be employed against a foreign power or be used to eliminate internal opposition.

A broad range of tactics are associated with politically motivated violence. These include selective violence directed against those whose activities are deemed to be crucial to the functioning of the state and its institutions such as politicians, police officers, soldiers and members of the judiciary. Violence may also be of an indiscriminate nature directed against the general public in a random fashion, seeking to intimidate the public which then exerts pressure on the government to give in to the demands of those carrying out such actions. Violence may also be directed at economic targets, seeking to subject the government to pressure from economic and commercial interests to concede to those using violence in order to prevent the further destruction of their property. The tactics of kidnapping, hijacking and robbery may be used to secure various ends, including raising money, securing publicity, discrediting the government or obtaining concessions.

see also...

Colonialism; State

Third way

The term 'third way' was increasingly used in the late 1990s to describe the ideology underpinning the actions of a number of socialist parties. It embraced the goals of opportunity and social inclusion based on support for capitalism. Many social democratic parties in Europe (such as the United Kingdom Labour Party and the German Social Democratic Party) shifted towards the 'third way' during this period

The first way was the approach of new right governments of the 1980s. The emphasis they placed on the free market intensified social divisions. Much of the wealth that had been created had not been invested, which meant that it had failed to percolate throughout society and instead, had created an 'underclass' who felt themselves to be permanently excluded from society, deprived of work, power and prospects. The second way consisted of social democracy, which placed considerable importance on nationalisation of key industries and public utilities.

The third way sought to retain private ownership but to rehape the way in which it worked by seeking to combine a company's responsibilities to its shareholders with responsibility to the wider community, including its customers, the workers it employed and the localities in which it operated.

The third way was underpinned by stakeholding which was directed towards the pursuit of social justice and the provision of wider opportunities for all within a market economy. It sought to equip individuals with the skills and capacities necessary to succeed in the highly flexible and constantly changing labour markets of modern capitalism but could also be depicted as a reform that was essential to the smooth operation of a market economy. A dynamic market required flexibility that was hindered by a permanently excluded underclass. The stakeholder economy was thus an approach that would provide for economic efficiency at the same time as dispensing a measure of social justice.

see also...

Collectivism; Individualism; New right; Social democracy; Socialism; Underclass

Third world

The term third world was initially used during the Cold War to denote a number of new nation states (initially in Asia and Africa and later in Latin America) that were in neither the Soviet or western blocs. Its subsequent use refers to countries that are economically underdeveloped in the sense of having a low level of industrialisation and a consequent high level of poverty and social problems such as illiteracy. A considerable number of them were former colonies of European nations. Although these subsequently gained their political independence from colonial rule they remained economically and culturally dependent on their former colonial masters. The term 'developing countries' is often used in preference to 'third world' since the latter term conveys the impresssion of countries with a low status in the world order.

Third world countries exhibit a vast range of social, economic and political differences. Many are predominantly agricultural societies, although mining may figure in the economies of some of them. Industry is frequently foreign owned, locating in third world countries as they seek to take advantage of factors such as the ability to pay low wages. The conditions of poverty in these countries (which exists even where, as in Mexico, considerable industrialisation has occurred) is compounded by the high level of debt owed to the industrialised world. There are, however, exceptions. The oil-producing states of the Middle East are rich and possess considerable influence on the world political stage, while a number of countries in the Pacific Rim (such as South Korea and Taiwan) have a relatively high level of industrialisation. The political arrangements in third world countries are also varied, although liberal democratic political systems in which there is a genuine competition for power among political parties and in which a wide range of civil liberties exist are rare. Many possess oligarchic political systems that are unstable.

see also...

Civil rights; Colonialism; Communism; Dependency; Liberal democracy; Totalitarian

Totalitarian

A totalitarian political system is one in which the state controls every aspect of the political, social, cultural and economic life of its citizens. It is governed by a ruling elite whose power is based upon ideological control that is exerted over the masses underpinned by the use of coercive methods. Civil liberties, human rights and the ability of citizens to participate in decision making are very limited if not totally absent in such societies. The term 'authoritarian' applies to societies that are also governed by an elite with considerable power, although this is not always exerted over every aspect of civil life, as is the case with totalitarianism.

The ideology found in totalitarian societies is subject to wide variation. Marxism–Leninism ideology dominated the former Soviet Union which was totally under the control of the Communist Party of the Soviet Union. Its leading members exerted control over institutions such as trade unions, the media and the military but alsoover key state-provided services such as education. Other totalitarian regimes may be dominated by the ideology of fascism in which only one political party is permitted to exist and representative institutions such as directly elected legislatures are typically absent. Totalitarian regimes may also be based on a religious ideology. Examples exist in Iran and in those areas of Afghanistan governed by the Taliban, where Sharia law is enforced, Islamic religious leaders occupy prominent political positions and political parties function in accordance with the *Koran* and Sharia. A main feature of theocratic government is its intolerance of viewpoints other than those of the dominant religious sect.

Totalitarian regimes differ from oligarchic ones. An oligarchy is a political system in which power is held by a small group of people who govern in their own interests rather than seeking to advance a political ideology. These interests may be economic or may consist of the desire to wield power.

see also...

Civil rights; Communism; Fascism; Human rights; Marxism–Leninism; Third world

Underclass

The term underclass applies to those on the bottom rung of the social ladder. There is no accepted definition of its meaning. The term was originally applied to the position of racial minorities: in the United Kingdom, they were marginalised by not being fully incorporated into the welfare state which accorded other members of the working class access to a range of rights and privileges such as employment, housing and social services. These were denied to ethnic minorities or allocated in a discriminatory fashion. In the late 1980s and early 1990s this term was redefined and is broadly applied in one of two ways providing it with either a cultural or a structural meaning.

In cultural terms the underclass has been depicted as a group of people demonstrating social behaviour that is at variance with the conduct of other, 'normal', members of society. It is seen to consist of people making the wrong moral choices. Their behaviour is particularly characterised by illegitimacy, involvement in crime (especially violent crime) and unemployment. The main cause of such pathological behaviour is attributed to the operations of social policy which encouraged immoral choices and absolved individuals from any blame for the consequences of their actions. The prime culprit for this cultural malaise was suggested to be the culture of dependency.

Structural definitions of the underclass asserted the importance of unemployment: the underclass consists of the economically unproductive, the unemployed and the unemployable. This emphasis on conditions as opposed to behaviour attributed the existence of the underclass to the operations of society and, in particular, to the extent of inequality. In the United Kingdom, particular blame was placed on the policies associated with Margaret Thatcher (born 1925) after 1979. Those who were unable ever to find jobs in post-industrial society and thus share in its rewards or prospects were treated as 'unwanted' (in the sense of being irrelevant to the process of production).

see also...

New right; Racism

Unitary system of government

A unitary system of government describes a political structure in which power is centralised in the hands of the national government. No other unit of government within the state possesses autonomous powers. Countries including Britain, Sweden and France possess such arrangements. This situation is contrasted with a federal system of government (as exists in Germany and America) in which power is divided between the central government and sub-national units. These are termed '*Länder*' in Germany and 'states' in America.

The main advantage of a unitary system of government is that when power resides at the centre it is possible for an elected government to be able to carry out its electoral promises unimpeded by the resistance that sub-national units of government may offer. A key difficulty with this system is that central government may become overbearing and ignore the feelings in specific localities that may be opposed to their policies. This may fuel separatist feelings and legitimise violence by those seeking independence from a central government that is viewed as oppressive or uncaring.

However, unitary states often possess a unit of government that is intermediate between national and local government. These are usually regional bodies providing services for a relatively wide geographic area whose inhabitants share some form of common identity such as language, culture or race. Regional authorities vary according to the autonomy they possess. Some exercise power that is devolved from national government thus giving them a wide degree of control over such delegated responsibilities. For example, regional authorities in Spain (termed autonomous communities) exercise a considerable degree of control over regional affairs. Others merely function as administrative bodies whose role is to provide regional services according to guidelines laid down by national government.

see also...

Devolution; Federal system of government; Mandate; Power; Sovereignty

Further reading

Ian Adams, *Political Ideology Today*, (Manchester: Manchester University Press, 1993). Although a little dated, this provides a useful account of the evolution and subsequent development of a wide range of political ideologies.

Alan Ball and B. Guy Peters, *Modern Politics and Government*, (Basingstoke: Macmillan, 2000 sixth edition). This is an ideal, up-to-date book for those with some existing knowledge of the subject area.

Michael Dummett, *Principles of Electoral Reform*, (Oxford: Oxford University Press, 1997). This book assesses what an electoral system is designed to achieve and provides detailed accounts of the operations of a wide range of them.

Andrew Heywood, *Political Ideas and Concept, An Introduction*, (Basingstoke: Macmillan, 1997). This is one of the best texts dealing with the study of political theories and ideas and is written in an easy-to-understand style.

Peter Joyce, *An Introduction to Politics*, (London: Hodder and Stoughton, 1999). This book is directed at those with little or no knowlege of politics and is written for those studying the subject at 'A' level or on first year undergraduate courses. Also directed at readers who are commencing their study of politics in the same author's *Teach Yourself Politics*. A second edition of this book is in preparation and will be published by Hodder and Stoughton in 2001.

Jurg Steiner, *European Democracies*, (Harlow: Longman, 4th edition). This provides an informative account of the operations of government in a number of European countries.

Also available in the series

TY 101 Key Ideas: Astronomy	Jim Breithaupt	0 340 78214 5
TY 101 Key Ideas: Buddhism	Mel Thompson	0 340 78028 2
TY 101 Key Ideas: Ecology	Paul Mitchell	0 340 78209 9
TY 101 Key Ideas: Evolution	Morton Jenkins	0 340 78210 2
TY 101 Key Ideas: Existentialism	George Myerson	0 340 78152 1
TY 101 Key Ideas: Genetics	Morton Jenkins	0 340 78211 0
TY 101 Key Ideas: Linguistics	Richard Horsey	0 340 78213 7
TY 101 Key Ideas: Philosophy	Paul Oliver	0 340 78029 0
TY 101 Key Ideas: Physics	Jim Breithaupt	0 340 79048 2
TY 101 Key Ideas: Psychology	Dave Robinson	0 340 78155 6
TY 101 Key Ideas: World Religions	Paul Oliver	0 340 79049 0